b i r d l a n d

Kathy McTavish

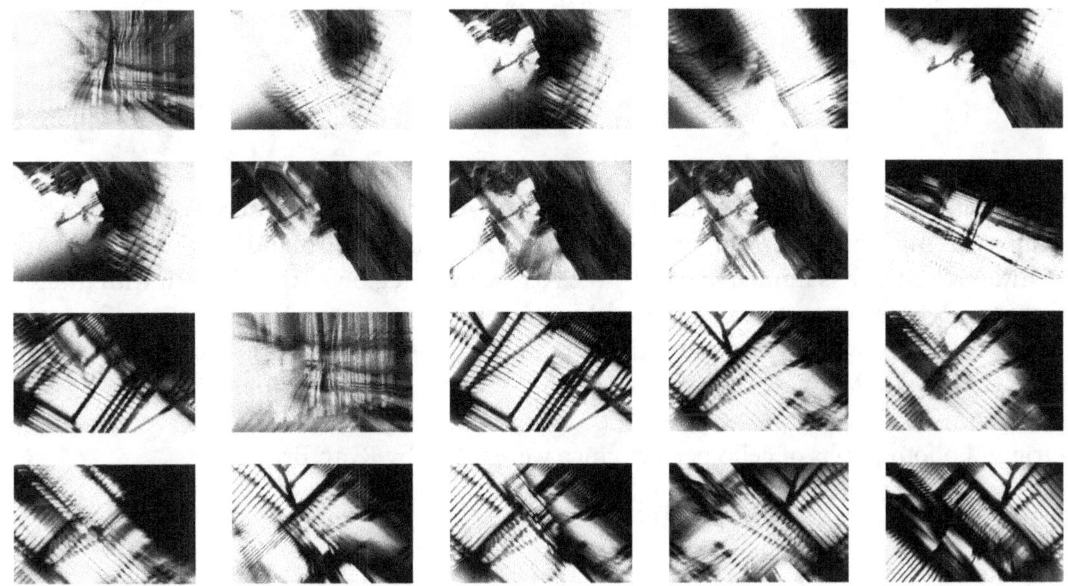

birdland
© 2011 Kathy McTavish
All rights reserved

Wildwood River Press
1748 Wildwood Road
Duluth, MN 55804
www.wildwoodriver.com

Printed in the United States
ISBN: 978-0-9843777-5-6
Library of Congress Control Number: 2011944529

for

Sheila Packa,

Donald & Janet McTavish,

Ruth McTavish,

& my cello

with love

I am grateful to the Jerome Foundation and the American Composers Forum for their support of my work. As a companion to the 2012 exhibit, "birdland" at the Duluth Art Institute, this book is funded in part by the Arrowhead Regional Arts Council with money from the Minnesota Arts and Cultural Heritage fund as appropriated by the Minnesota State Legislature with money from the vote of the people of Minnesota on November 4, 2008. Thank you Minnesota!

Original photographs of cello performance were taken by Ryan Braski.

"love, love, how grief rises into dark stars ..."
Sheila Packa

contents

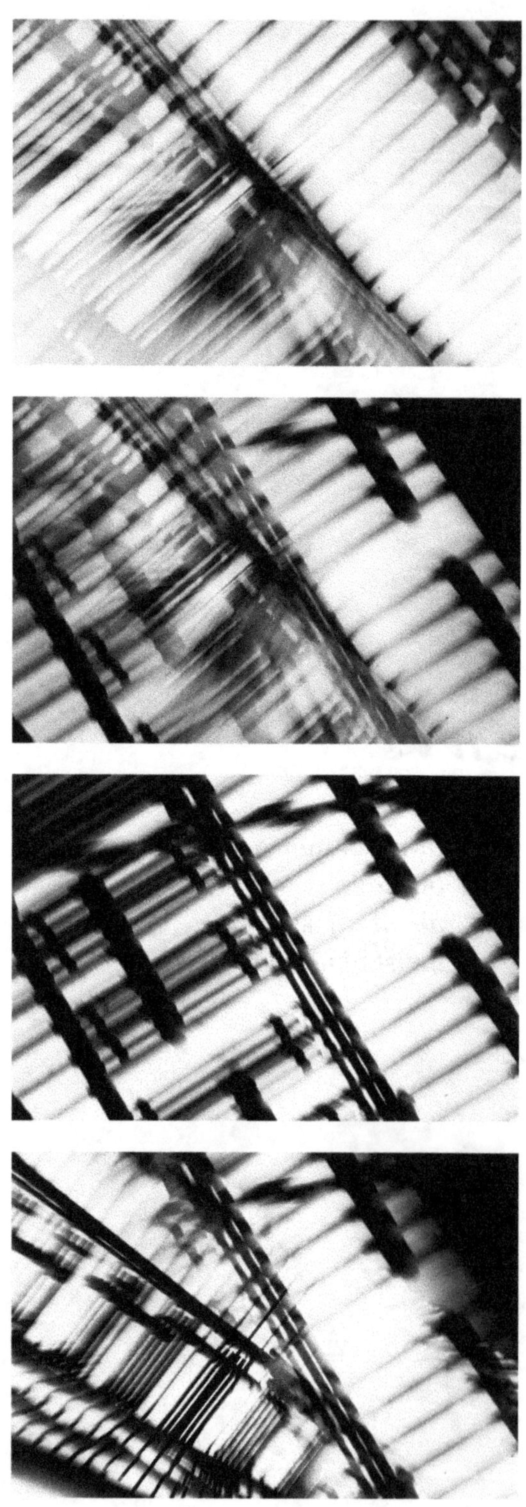

introduction

Kathy McTavish told me: "You can never know where creative work is going to lead. If you listen really hard, something emerges. When that something emerges, you just know it. You can feel it. The work has spoken to you or something has spoken through the work. For me, this is a cross-sensory experience. I can hear the image, I can see the sound. It takes a life of its own. You know at that point you are physically part of the work creating itself. It's unmistakable."

The cello is her center, and now her work in music has extended to writing and film. She bends notes, transposes image, and studies light. On her cello, she plays the dark hour in the house, eyes closed. She starts on a ladder. The friction of the bow traveling across wires could start a fire. She has a certain horsepower. The red-bellied instrument leans against her breast bone. She listens to the pegs and scroll, listens to the pouring of a river down the slope, and she rides unknown winds.

Her work, a blend of composition and improv, is called deep listening. The composer Pauline Oliveros used this phrase to describe a deep attentiveness to the moment. Kathy McTavish's creativity is based on her deep attentiveness — her cello is both a resonant and responsive instrument that draws the listener into its sound. Her work triggers an invisible procession of images like those in this poem by Cavafy:

God Forsakes Antony

When suddenly, at midnight, you hear
an invisible procession going by
with exquisite music, voices,
don't mourn your luck that's failing now ...

...
listen — your final delectation — to the voices,
to the exquisite music of that strange procession,
and say goodbye to her, to the Alexandria you are losing.

Constantine P. Cavafy (1911)
Translated by Edmund Keeley and Philip Sherrard

Always the cello, the callouses on her fingertips exploring the harmonics, and the bow sliding over notes above and below the bridge. Sometimes she taps the chamber inside that holds the deepest shadow, where no light goes. She draws out longing and grief and fastens them to the light falling from the window.

No surprise — she too has an invisible procession of images made manifest with her camera. Like her cello, the camera becomes an instrument for improvisational work. The blurred photographs with their composition of lines and color are abstract and evocative. She has leaned over each one with careful attention, creating frame by frame a still-motion film, a moving abstract expressionist painting.

In an interview, when asked how she begins, she says, *somewhere.* This doesn't mean anywhere. Each room has its own ambience, echo and vibration; if we listen, we can hear it too. She starts with becoming resonant with the room. Sounds that come in do not interrupt the flow but became embraced, echoed, embellished. She has a receptivity, an openness to sound that extends beyond the ordinary bounds of music. She uses found sound: a coffee pot, the cry of a bird, the creak of a hinge, wheels on the pavement or the Empire Builder rolling along the tracks from here to Seattle and to the Pacific Ocean. She makes another world, a strange city, an ocean with heavy surf, stones rolling on the beach, and whales migrating.

The music and image come together here in this book, *Birdland.* It is a score. The normal mapping of musical notes onto manuscript paper does not express her work, but this book comes close.

The long poem sequence of *Birdland* is another language for what she says in her music and film. It evokes the song "Birdland" by Patti Smith and echos the beat poets. Like the song by Patti Smith, it explores a connection with a father. The boy becomes a raven. It is transgender. It is an Allen Ginsberg-like howl. The story begins with a bird over a landscape of America, over cities, industry, roads. The story begins in zero person, or in the persona of the cello, and embraces the homeless and the strangers who wander the streets, goes into a practice room in North Carolina to a hospital ward to a man bending circuits to a factory to waking up it-was-like-this-every-morning to a city at night. There are characters like Night Crow No Time and River Icarus which reference songs on a previous album. It has a strange music. The cello resounds within it.

Kathy McTavish has a background in ecology and theoretical mathematics. In science, she was fascinated by patterns — these patterns have become her art. Here is a dynamical ecosystem that is either dying or rising. Deeply emotional and sensitive, her lines are on a canvas sky, all of it changing. Her work is music, it is visual art, it is sound art, found objects, and motion.

Instead of multimedia, implying separate threads, her work is trans-media. This genre-bending artist plays image and words as if they were music and paints music as if she were creating visual art. In photography, the bokeh effect (originally named by a few Japanese photographers) brings the attention away from the object itself to the rhythms of its design. The photographs are of an urban environment: here are fire escapes, ladders, windows, and streets. There are layers used over and beneath. She has a sensitive geometry of lines and grids that always find the light.

She uses blur in all her work. At first it can be disorienting, pulling the listener away from the fixed tracks of ordinary music into places with no map. Expectation is up-ended; she takes the threads of the past and travels into the territory of the present moment surging across a vast landscape. She transposes to one form and then another. She creates dreams of a dying planet, an unknown city, and a wandering journey. The frames slip. The transitions dissolve and everything becomes bridge.

One of her favorite places to play is at Sacred Heart Music Center on First Street in Duluth, an old neighborhood near low rent buildings sided with asphalt, suffering from years of neglect, fire escapes made of two by fours, and peopled by vibrant young people with baby carriages and expensive electronics. The old church is west of the old Washington Junior High School across from the Damiano Center soup kitchen and next to the Center for American Indian Resources. It is now de-sanctified but has new life as concert venue. Going to hear her play last year, I pulled the vertical bar on the eight foot door to go inside. Stained glass windows let in the weak winter light, the walls are a grimy white, the ceiling is held up by columns that become Roman arches, shaped like a bishop's hat. In the corners, a pile of unused lumber and some trash. The floors, once a beige flecked linoleum tile broken and spongy with damp, have been replaced by a polished oak. Before, to walk across the floor was to feel the sway and trembling, as if one were crossing a rope bridge over a gorge. I listen to her unlatch the latches of the ebony case, lift the deep red instrument, warm up.

Vestiges of a former splendor, dark bronze chandeliers suspended above with clear white lights, a massive balcony with a pipe organ, a confessional with its burgundy velvet curtain drawn closed. On the right, a women's room, a former sacristy with its own stained glass windows. The church was built before indoor bathrooms. In a stall, above the porcelain toilet, the stained glass window features a book, holy but blank, perhaps waiting to be written. At the front of Sacred Heart is an altar. The floor mosaic is a geometry of one-inch tiles in white, blue and sage and crimson that pattern two risers to the elevation of the altar. It feels like the surround of an aqua swimming pool from the 1920s where women in rubber caps swam in synchrony. At the front, the white altar is made of marble, dusty, stripped of the gold chalice, candlesticks and incense burners. There is no longer a crucifix, only one thing, a wrought iron heart lit with red votive candles. She plays softly at first as if the sounds were flickering like the candles, and then the cello rises and lifts the arches.

I listen to notes that she swept aside, as if she were ahead of some developing text. Her film is a score. The camera is the saxophone of John Coltraine, improv with stills. She sequences endless notes and angles of light. She finds beauty in made objects, even those that are broken. She decodes the industrial genome. Ladders. Metalwork. Radiators. Pipes. Faucets. Drains. Mesh. Grids, spans. Spider webs. Window panes. Sidewalks. Oblique angles on the linear. Bricks, doors, overhead beams. An urban decay. Rust. Lime deposits.

Silt, dust, grit. I remember its light today, yesterday, the day before, yards more light, miles. Her eyes are closed as if what she plays is written inside. The music folds around like sheets and reaches a wide space. Feathers fall. There's a bending, an empty chamber, leaves in the wind. In the sound of strings, a distance both near and far.

The long poem here meets the images and becomes a score for the music. It takes grief and longing and connects it to the mystical. It leans against the frames, becomes a magnifying glass. The focal point shifts as do the lines of perspective. The eye of the camera takes in both near and far simultaneously. It enters the sound spaces she's created. Her writing is a hYmn to the journey.

Sheila Packa
November 2011

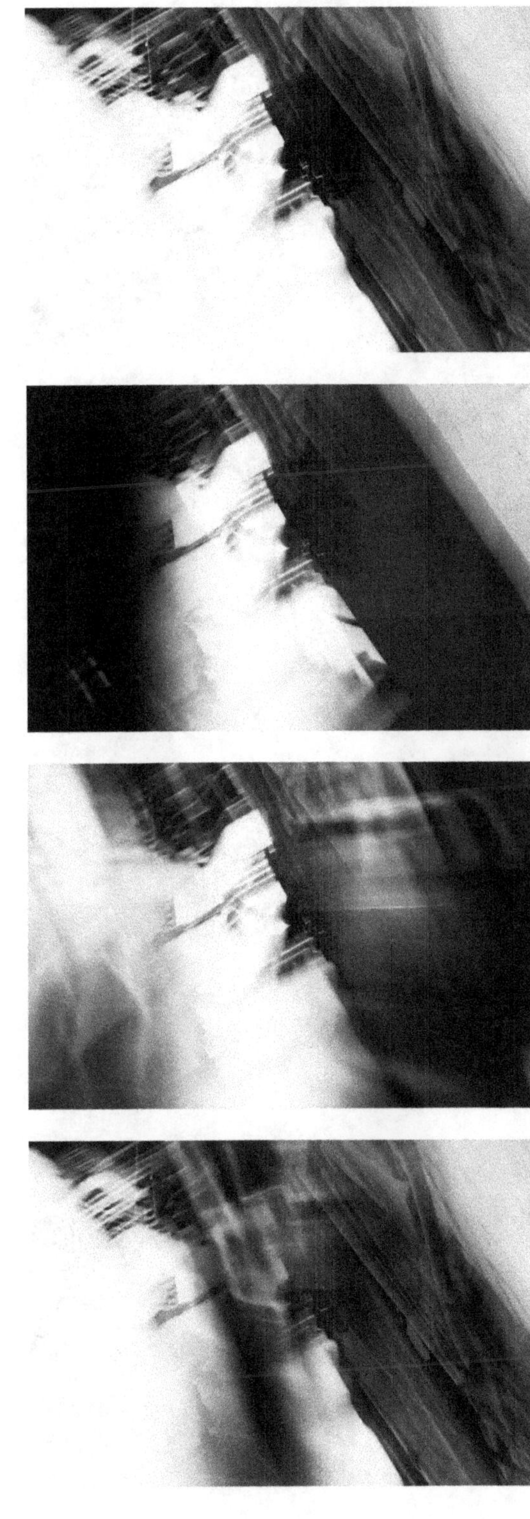

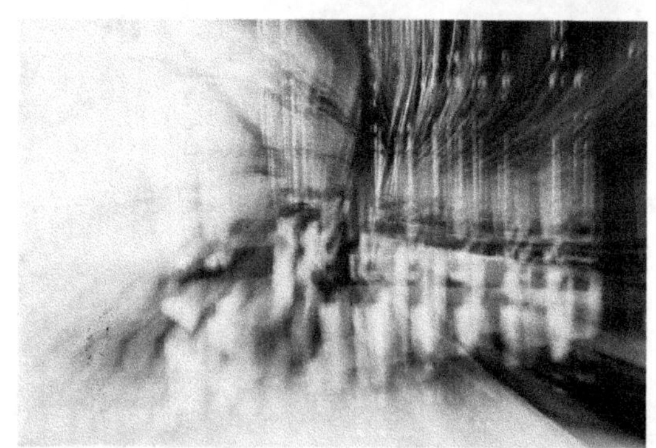

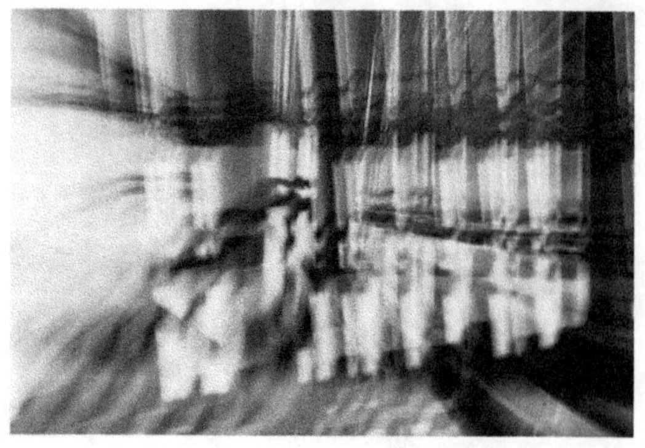

birdland

ЖƷπØπƷЖ

my hands were made of
bone & pulsing sound
i was a red wagon
black crow / blue bottle

ЖƷπØπƷЖ

dark wings
beat 3 times
& then
a queer
suspension
darkness &
pin hole
illuminations
no landmarks
no compass
tracks, roads
intersecting webs
rivers —

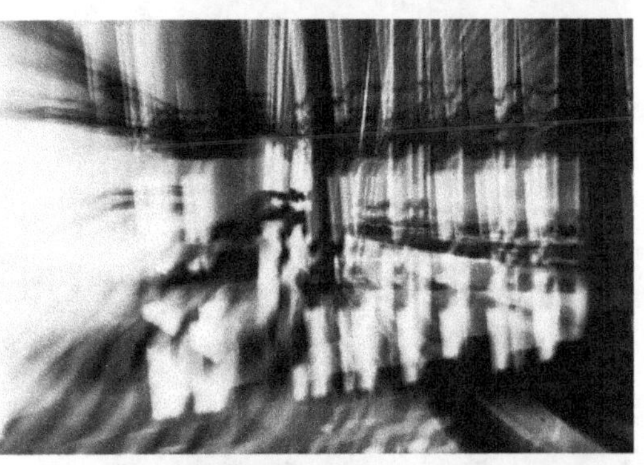

a rushing turbulence
a sinew & pulse
dark marrow
blood & barren plains
shadow, spun rock & fire
an iron railing
& time
seas rise
boats capsize
swallow water

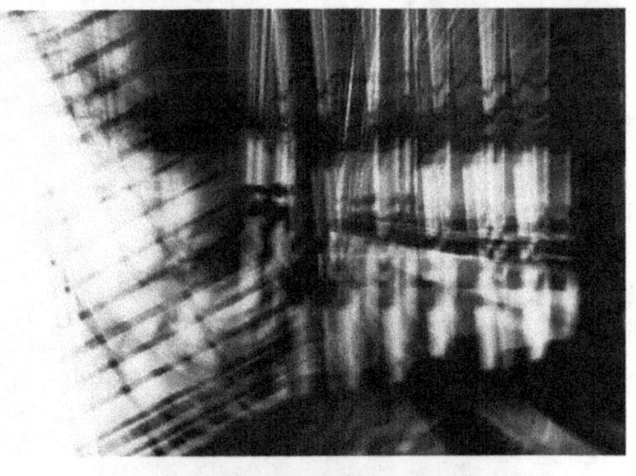

turn & drown
dark waves erase
the passage
down
there were lights above
unmoved
while lamps below
flickered & burned
vast & deep
broken glass

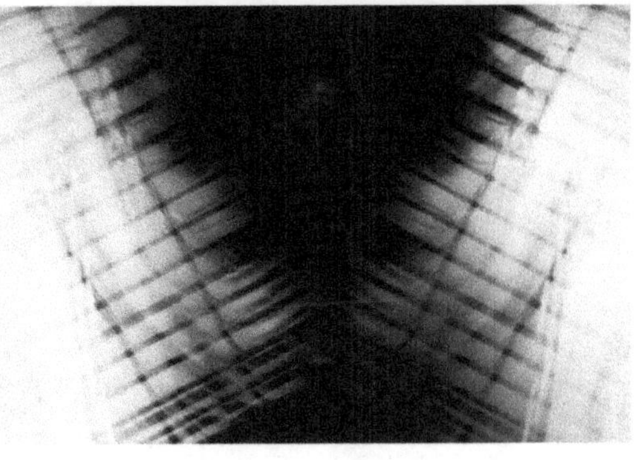

stitched into dark blankets
of sleep
rocks aged
cyclones circled
a bird's
slate eye

Ж⋺πØπ⋺Ж

raven feathers splayed
across the indigo cloud
beast or loom or cliff
a spider scales glacial walls
a radio tower pierces the sky
clouds gather
a transmission
low & hurried
static —
the machine itself
begins to speak
electrical pulse
vibrating plates of glass
wires intersecting
red, black, white
barbed wire transmission
an orchestra concert
from Royal Albert Hall
before the bombing
commercial interlude
blue coal, white appliance
red letters, steel borders
cargo train, trucks
& planes
knifelike wanderers
a sign, 2 roads
voyage of goods
to odessa
to new york
to madrid
to portland
past abandoned farms
fallen towns, rusted track

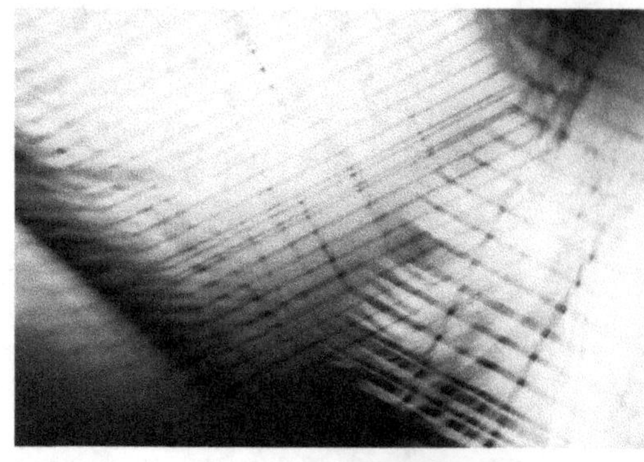
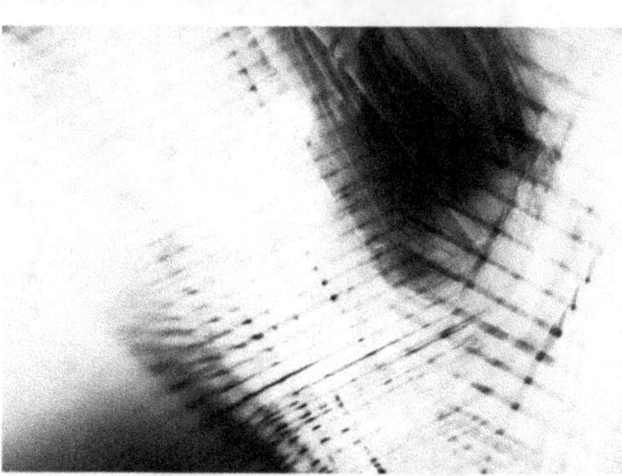
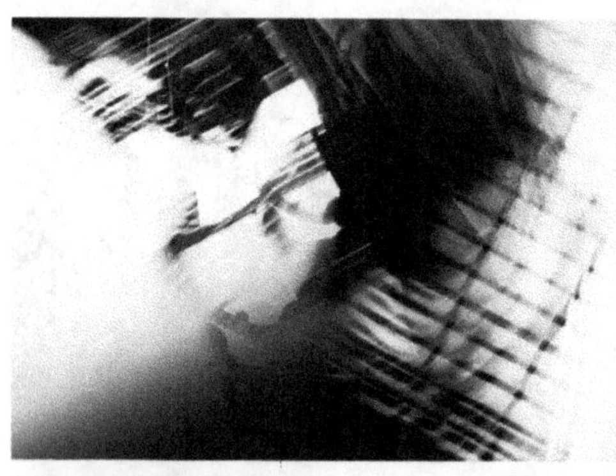
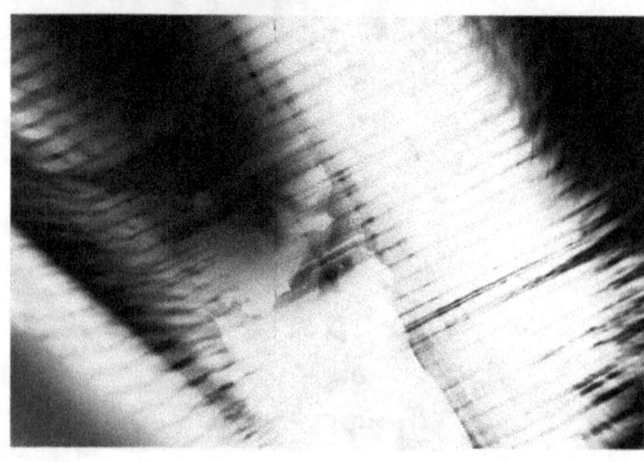

past incinerations
past temples & bars
iron horse, iron lung
combine turning
gold fields, blue smoke
under the high bridge
birds & ghosts
dusty hYmn
white gray
paint
concrete canvas
fallen feathers
splintered caws
a cavern of birds
ceiling of birds
bridge of birds
coat of birds, quick silver
cloak of birds
dark & trembling storm
the boats were green, blue, red
pale sails
anchors heavy
& iron & braided with sea
ropes
slowly plumbing the depths
anyway there was a map
industry!
progress!
we had a plan
we had time on a spool
or wires on a spool
or a snake skin with a map
or a spoon
we had a shiny spoon
a wheel & fire
machines, wheels, talking wires
fire
& lots of things to burn
rock & roll factory
spoons & knives
axes & lightning
lightning on a spool

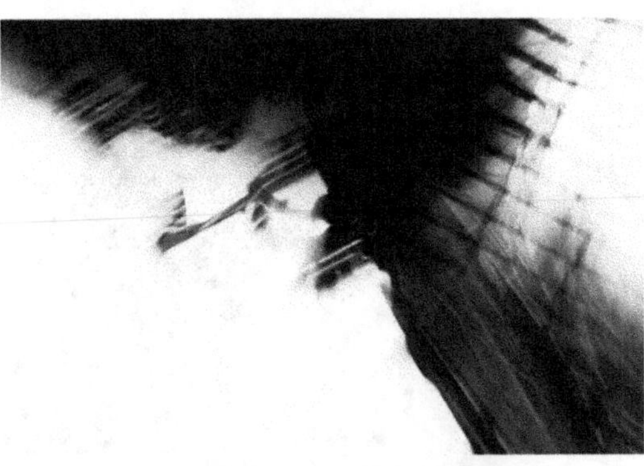

a voyage of goods
timetables & maps
& silver roads
silver snakes
& a rope
a pulley, a rope
a factory, a boat
a plane & sky
skyscrapers
windows like birds
higher than birds
higher than gods
high as stars
higher than stars
we had skyscrapers
& planes & windows
& stairs winding up past clouds
stairwells & lights & vast landscapes
of asphalt
roofscape, fire escape, flashlight
a stairwell, a window, a street
fires below & stars

Ж꓿πᎧπ꓿Ж

wings & dark mountain
shadow mountain — a cliff
perilously close
a breath, a moth
an illuminated distance
a stillness before raging nights
wind gathering force
a spring, a wheel
rain factory, sleet factory
lightning on telephone wires
gripping the kite — a static suspension
the key aflame
wings beating
toward shore
distant gray lines
taut heart beat swift

ЖϾпϾЖ

3 birds
laughing
whose last laugh?
3 birds, last bird, coughing bird
anyway the factory was going well
conveyer belts burning rubber
tires pulling freight past trees & signs
& swamps
highways, roads & concrete bridges
golden arches
music on the radio
a bottle of coke
the marlboro man
red & white package
tightly bound
white shirt sleeves
rolled up against the heat
a swollen heat, a humid sea
of green & gray & grit
radio smoke rings
smoke signals
drowsy black asphalt
yellow line

ЖϾпϾЖ

whispers
pulse
shadows moving
frozen hands
a clock
arctic stillness
ice
a blue darkness, chill gray
& steam through grates
a silence
chalk on slate
blue window
red chair, chrome feet
a fluorescence

stairs ascending
dim yellow light
dusty rays waking
tired sun
clouded
incandescent
sun
pull-chain-porcelain-filament
sun
it was like this every morning
same train
same chair
same window
same tap water drip
or brook
& rusted bridge
iced metal thrumming
same bus or concrete sidewalk
trash can alley
aluminum percolator
stained glass bulb
brown liquid
blue blue morning

ЖƆπØπƆЖ

chalk & black slate
a formula or system
deciphered
a bifurcation
group theory
a flaw in the arithmetic
vectors, differentials
copied into black books
a slight variation
parameters altered
a solution
sought
to simplify
3 things
hold up this space
a basis for turning

a transformation or mapping
find
a simpler set of lines
a stable state
a zero
or one

Ж⅂πØπ⅃Ж

people were saving daylight
small blue squares of light
small extinctions
3 then 2 then 1
rungs marked off in notches
fabric of millenniums
fossils really
carbon, feathers, muscle
then stone
an empty cage
a hollow ocean
but anyway
i liked color & light
the way shadows held a sound
textures, frictions
joining of pitch
horse hair & wire
scraped across the chest
eyes split by light
light hYmn
threads & loom & glass
broken places
a wooden room
resonance
box
echo chamber
hallways
old cathedrals
warehouse caverns
holy spaces
sound
a silo of birds
a bridge in flight

there was
a black & white
television
body counts
a black woman in flight
dogs, guns, iron bars
it sears
that picture
those words

Ж∋πØπ∋Ж

i always wanted to be my father
wooden hammer, wire nails
the smell of gasoline engines
wool shirt, boots
asphalt shingles
clamps & glue
old metal tackle box
hinges & screws
pliers & saw
a rasping sound
small town & farm
the smell of oats
factory of oats
river industry
warehouse & tracks

Ж∋πØπ∋Ж

blue bottle, wooden room
4 white plaster walls
worn building
a painter
a radiator
a sink

it was like this every morning
blue sky
pale sink
rusted drain
glass window

worn boots
city streets
waking
aluminum
coffee
percolator
gas flame
brown liquid
small
wooden room
4 white
plaster walls
blue bottle
gray cat
painted
iron
radiator

it was like this every morning
rain eyes
a window
sound tunnel
coffee
white steam

ЖƆπØπƆЖ

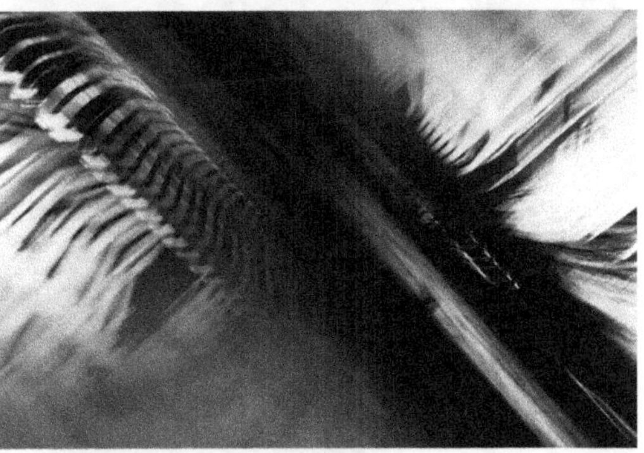

practice room, early light
rosin & morning
wood & light
fragile dusk
fleeting blue vision
hands in wool
worn boots
black jacket
walking
brown eyes
urban sky
shock of hair
wind or rain
black road
red thoughts

a line or thread
string or note
heart beat
pulse
vibration
sine waves
colliding
tides & winds
turbulence
rip tides
& gale winds
layers of blue
& friction
blue green pitch
plumb line
lost anchor
horizon
drowned
tilted
white foam
where sea
turned to sky
turned to planets
invisible orbits
slanted axis
mast & sail
3 moons
plankton & clouds
one lamp
turning

ЖꓷπøπꓷЖ

sound is produced
by the collision
of two bodies

ЖꓷπøπꓷЖ

there was a man
bending circuits
in the ancient barn

blacksmith of sound
with rope & pulley
wire gods
bending gravity
into light & heat
& pigeons rising
from blackened iron
black horses
concrete
& corrugated steel
direct current
clouds of horses
rain on steel
over battered stairs
frame & joints
in a crucifix
on thick blue glass
in the silo
a cyclone
of birds

ЖƎπØπƎЖ

sanctified x
hovering x
circling x
we were looking
for something
the post & beam
the underlying force
light or electricity
vector spaces
the basis
a fixed point
a dynamic or web
fluid or particles
our hands
our bodies reaching
the mind grasping
or releasing the failures
there was a vector space
an algebra

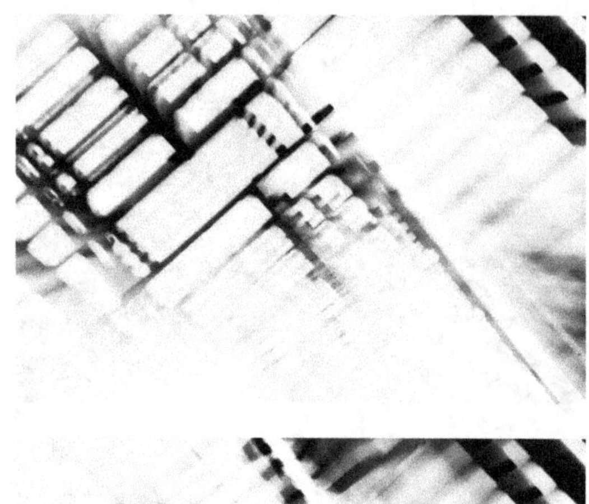

the senses struggling
with the mind
you could hear
a far away sound
a siren or hYmn or
evening light
angels & birds
clouds & horses
bees
vibrating ether
x
equals
light & electricity & silence
or light & pitch & rocks
or water & glass & iron
or noise particles colliding
not knowing
if it was simply
clusters of energy
inflection points
fixed states — a stillness
gravity pulling
poles repelling
webs colliding
the number zero
dancing
to a jukebox
on red
checker board floors
& beer signs
this radio, this night
gleaming neon & rain
reading the directions
seeing the signs
blue quaker king of oats
a book of stamps
cigarettes
broken kite
melted wax
quixotic flight
night crow scratching
lost translations

typing texts
black ink
parchment
a stone
scribbled texts
formulas, illustrations
footnotes, histories
calculations, page numbers
corner of the world
taco stand & map
we were there or
you are here
a location, a focal point
a certain depth of field
in the midst of
the vast eternity or
7 layers —
infinite skies
couldn't just count them
or it would take a long time
an uncountable number of years
to count the layers
so many possible answers
so many ways to measure things
to count the objects
to list the objects
& often they dissolved
into clusters of light
staining
the surface of things
in a radiance
that made you
lose count
lose your grip
forget the citation
a transfiguration
an illumination
that left you standing
with your heart
like a hat
in your hands
stammering

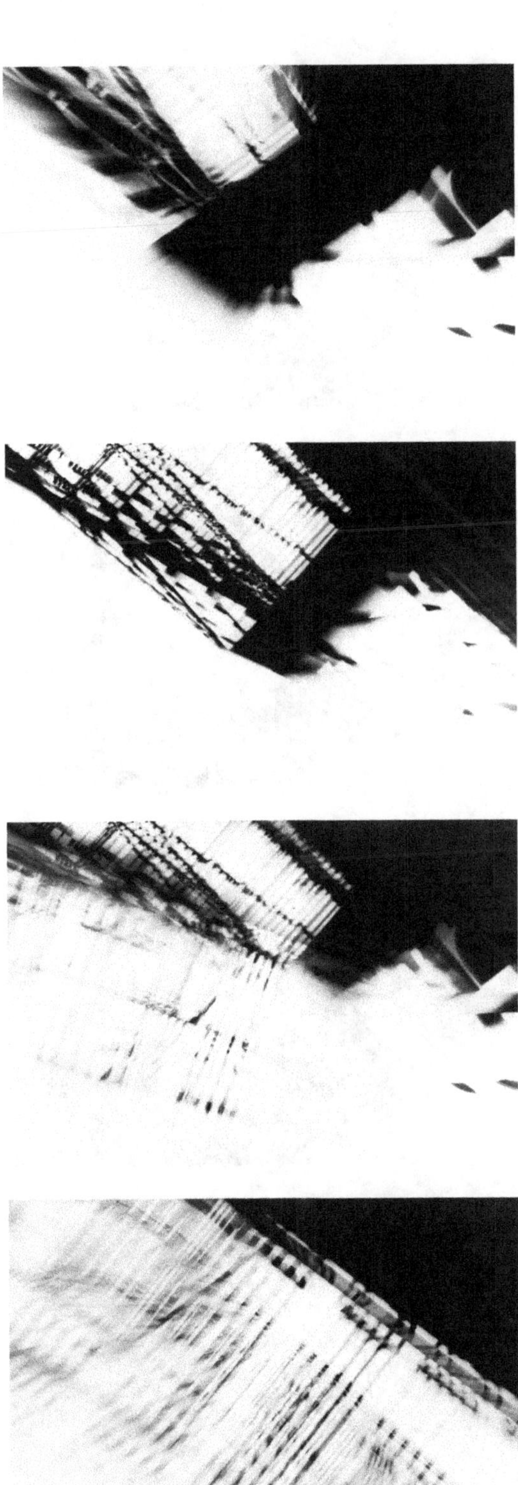

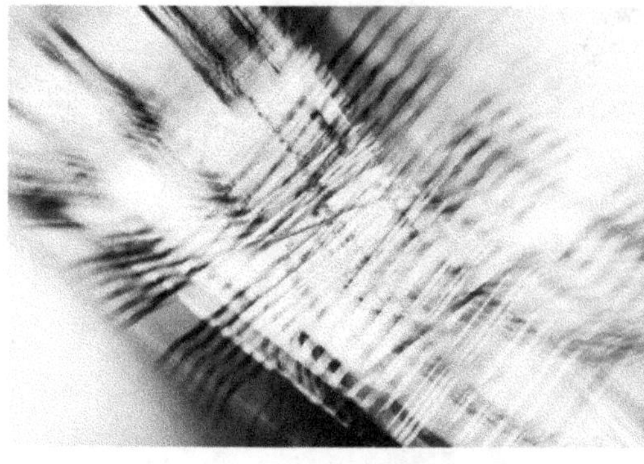

and the window of zero
irresistibly compelling
glorious sanctified
eyes of a crow

ЖϽπ⊘πϽЖ

red star
black night
or lucky strike &
bus stop midnight
if there were 2 or 3
they were ghosts
a rising city
endless flight
heart or sky or cloud
canvas or road
low blue smoke
a railroad track
stretching miles
across bog
& grass
& trees

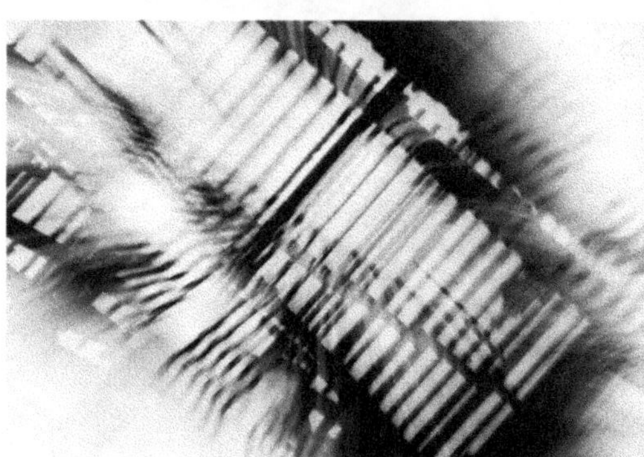

slowly reaching
dense fog
cattail & sedge
early morning or dusk
night drifting across the world
a bridge — still water
a hush
soundless turning
or wind listless through
yellowed grasses
history rising

a story winding past distant rails
a low vibration
past the heart
taut strings released
silent bird
lonely stream
last light
dark blade of water

night
black wing buried in clouds
echoed in rivers
an infinite & far away sound
broken & falling
hYmn of birds
far away ship & endless sea
adrift or in flight
the sea, the dusty sky
stained sea & bleeding sky
rising or falling
blue gray longing
reaching or belief
hYmn or wish
or cry or breathlessness
a sound or line or word
great heaving or loss
reaching towards vast ends of sea
haunted eyes
scar or wound or wing
echo & ghost
etched into caves or body
river eyes
the sea or boat or bridge
a road & sound like light
dusty light & window
glass or wire
silver nets, yellow fish
light gleaming
light threads
luminous
and haunted
not close but far
not far but here
in this room on this bridge
last bird
if we never had this place
emerald & blue
holy dream
cloud dream
or depths of sea
light drowning in layers of sea

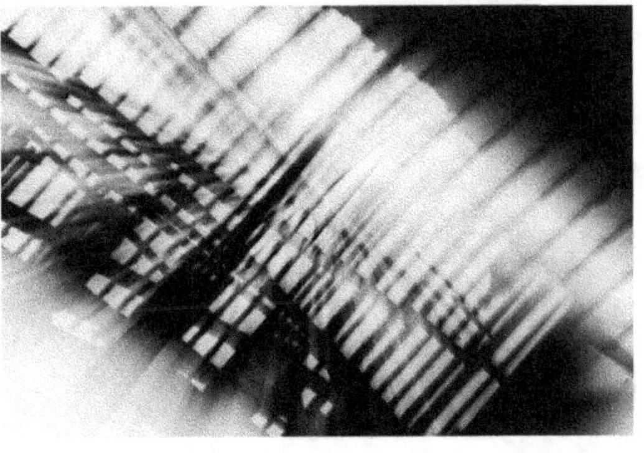

eyes straining through
murky depth
a dream of smoky bars
neon & rain
only ash
a cigarette lit or drowned
holy dream
holy redemption
i walked there
or i was stained
by that river that light
now this scar, this wound
holy imprint
a railroad track
& grasses
bending

Ж∋πⵁπ∋Ж

luminous failures
wax wings & falling
an orchestration or book
film or loom
or simply a crow
& shiny red wrapper
degenerate opera
endless screeching
scraping sounds
& pitch salvaged
from an auto junkyard
forgotten words
torn bits of labels
abandoned bottles

Ж∋πⵁπ∋Ж

in fields of sage
whistle &
drowned rhythm
wheels, tracks &
pistons turning
an iron bird calling

through brown
sagebrush, yellowed stalks
limestone & flooded earth
heavy snows / late spring
flooded tracks
gray horse
cloistered rider
fallen stones & rusted silos
industrial wasteland
abandoned warehouse
fossilized grain
skeletons of steel
vast plains of destruction
raging forces
empty husks
industrial cyclones
& rusted dreams
cattle strewn across
devastated plains
& lost souls clutching
suitcases
battered, frayed
broken masts & shopping carts
dark & empty malls
hollow ringing vacant
vast & violent sea

ЖꙄπØπꙄЖ

red shirt
black hair
slender blade
night-laced trembling streets
shadow of crow
window or sidewalk
boot lace & worn denim
edge of drainpipe
black with soot
red with rust
white slice of neon
cloudy night
drop of rain / dusty glass

ЖƎπØπƎЖ

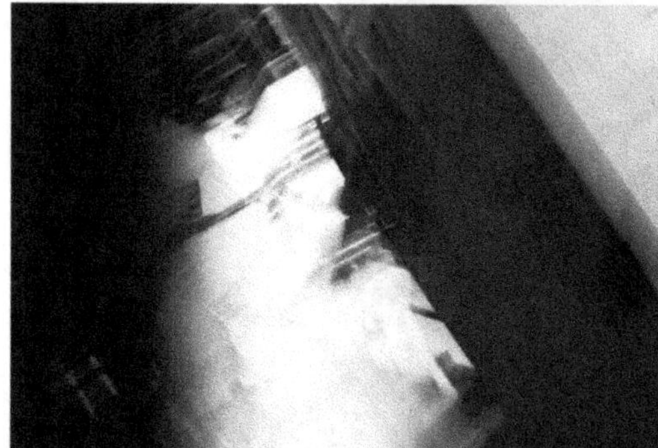

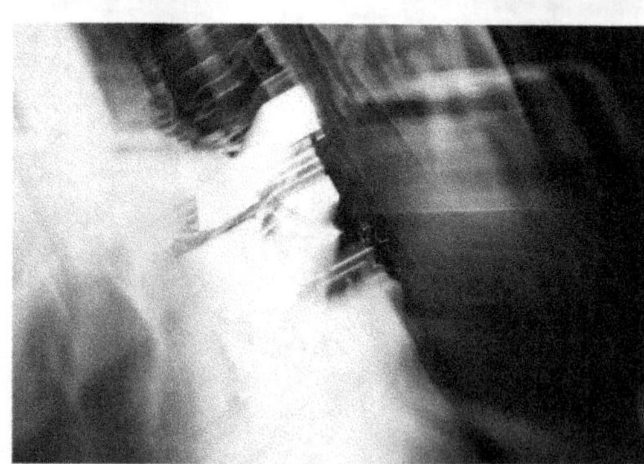

green monastery
or cloud
damp blue mist
gray silence
black rock
jagged white mineral line
memory or place
near depths
shadow canyons
blades of light
dusty filaments
taut lumens
holy dissonance
chords of silence
hallowed bridge
web of light & green
& stone & rivers
spilling across forest floors
& rocky cliffs
trees lifting past lifetimes
into infinite blue nights
the bendability of time
the synthesis
of rock & sun into
green & sinew
transmigration of mineral
& water
shadow & light
a fluid dynamic
a cluster of cells
electric photo
transmissions
criss cross of
migrating elements
shape shifting forms
elemental forces
bound, fused & released
makers of air
air looms
weaving invisible ribbons

falling maps
marked by temporary arteries
monastic green tent
ocean of birds

ЖƧπØπƧЖ

my hands were made of
bone & pulsing sound
i was a red wagon
black crow / blue bottle
suspended
between sound & water
or notes & sidewalk
there was a word for it
but it was far away
& people kept moving
bridges arched above
silver streams /
rushing cars
loud / relentless /
tunnel
sound & gravity /
echo
metallic scream

ЖƧπØπƧЖ

a moth throws herself
into the closest street lamp
lines transect darkness
into silver threads
voices along wire webs
float into stars
the world grows close
human rivers dry up
into 3 strangers
gaunt & worn
frayed & dissolute
mapless wanderers
with sandwiches or hope
seeking mission signs

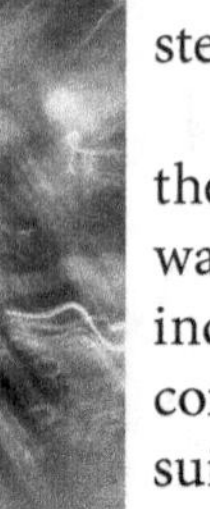
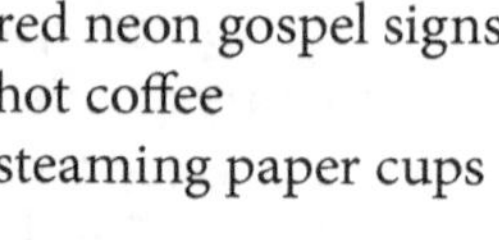

red neon gospel signs
hot coffee
steaming paper cups

the cool night
washes away
industry
commerce
suits & deals
angels mend wings
in dimly lit bus shelters
jesus saves!
the endless circle fades
death all around us
whales & bees
& mary / red heart
& outstretched hands
blue veil
blue blue sky
an alchemy of blue
one last bird
electric wires
& sea

ЖꓱπØπꓱЖ

language of knot & stone
language of birds
shadow, cloud & wire
electric filaments
night's blue lantern
flux & green mist
white horse or silver cloud
angels & junkies
degenerate streets
artists of chaos
falling opera
broken book
wire quartet
groan of wood
snapped mast & waves
a mapless sea

red star weeping
dusty windows
thick plates of glass
an opening so slight
a vision so fleeting
only a line of chalk
or a crack in the world
a breath or glance or
fever
fallen feather
floating fish
wooden skeleton
& black ribbons
a ghostly day & arid noon
strobe-light sun
& asphalt steam

Ж∃π∅π∃Ж

watches for sale
broken hYmn
broken planet
sirens of commerce
one last bird
& sea

Ж∃π∅π∃Ж

birds / no birds
there was a river with no birds
no black raven
there was a river with gleaming birds
green & blue shore
no river
no vibrant threads
no shore, no trees

a hole in the sky
a heart or bird or door
broken window / fallen glass
& sky
silver fall

keening hYmn
broken hYmn
icarus & luminous flight
a low & broken sound
dream of life
no sky, no planet, no dream
radio pluto

graffiti music

river icarus
wanderer icarus
traversals
by boat, on foot
in dreams, by train
a bridge
& water & sky
a body
broken wings
a gender, a bird
a sound, 4 strings
a boat
wool coat
& wind
relentless
force

Ж-ЭпⵁпЭЖ

always before tomorrow
low siren calls
below the surface
some moment in history
unfolding, relentless
human tide

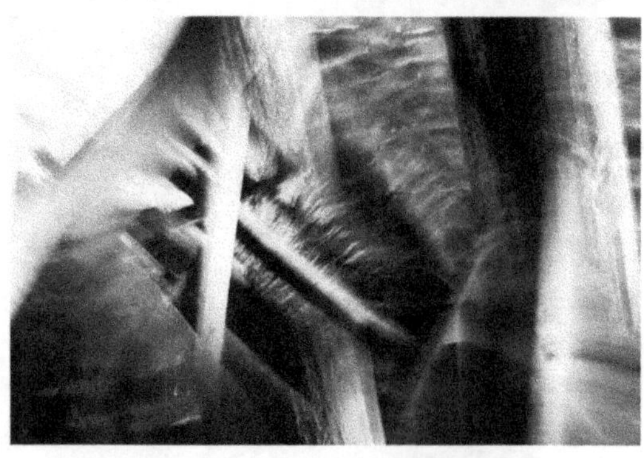

Ж-ЭпⵁпЭЖ

resistance
something frayed
a friction
a tension

something broken
jagged torn fragmented
razed

ЖꙄπØπꙄЖ

close & blurred
zero person
not first, not second, not third
no map, no compass, no horizon
ephemeral imprint
sound & sand & rainfall
notes blown about
& dissipating
notes streaming
notes rising
falling
in corners silence
driftless / shady
deep pools
harmonic ghosts
suspended in clouds
across the moon
tonal palette
note clusters
probability clouds
gravitational forces
continuous dynamics
sound webs
rugged terrains
orthogonal chords
a calculus of motion
the dynamics of waves
residue of ghosts
a river
etched into rock
a glacial stain
cave drawings
subway icarus
railway icarus
river icarus
glassy fires

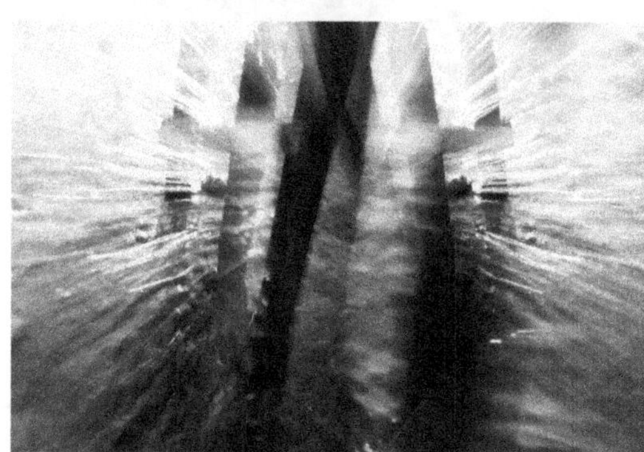

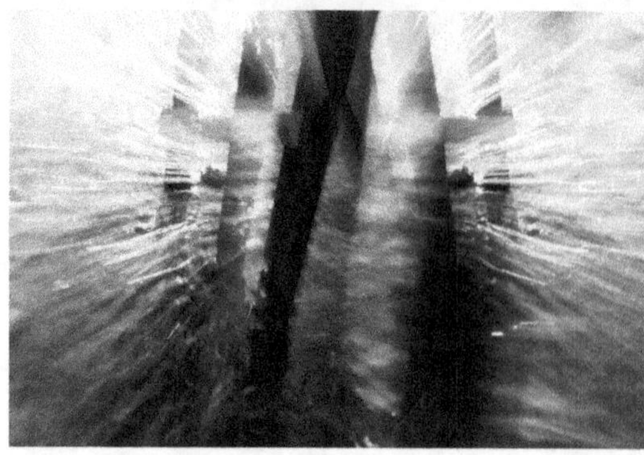

rain & cold
rush of color
sound & city
gleaming city
trumpet city
alley night
hidden streets
darkened streets
starry night
sheets of rain & neon
not a lattice
but notes falling
& dissolving
ghosts
wind & shadow
river bridge
improv planes
free jazz
no map
immersion, risk, lost & hOwl
infinite between
unbound netherworld
harmonic bird
tonal bird
falling
friction
gods of chance
dark wings
dissonant hYmns
dusty light
threads of light
submerged
gray shadows
illuminated
ladders & & . . .
graffiti tunnel
radio pluto
stereo fields
resonance / reverberation
twisted & splintered
lines bent
& sea's depth

cave drawings
black & red
ink sky
endless sky
horses speak to sky

ЖƎπØπƎЖ

i often played in bars

working people
musicians
poets
inebriated
intoxicated
otherworldly
mesmerized
played the
wooden beast
wild bird
tin cup
drunken utterances
stuttered offerings
thick strings
piercing hOwl
a matter of tension
clouds & cyclones
pierced night
prophets
dark & bitter
liquid dreams
fistfuls of change
folded paper
feathers
sketches
poems
gifts from strange angels

dark & smoky bars

ЖƎπØπƎЖ

between
a vast landscape
sparse or dense
infinite between
a silence
clouds
rain
particles
cluster & scatter
twist & rise
reverberate

ЖƎπØπƎЖ

i was 17
when i first
walked into a gay bar

small dark room
smoke & bottles
hands, eyes
sound
the room was
spinning
about some axis
warm & close
juke box sound & street
stained by rain
swimming & neon
late night dreaming
crimson laced
blue blue heart
awkward waltz
dark brown eyes
& hidden glances
pressed close
against
dark corners
slung low
across the night
queer
not a boy

not a girl
bird or tree
walking
pavement lit
street lamps
signs
neon
walking
river
bridge
sailor, waif, poet
lucky strike
red & black
concrete, brick
blue glass &
well-worn locks
the bird
scrawled
red & white & black
graffiti angel

ЖƎπƟπƎЖ

saxophone dreams
the man in the psych ward
drugged beyond recognition
close calls
i sang like a bird
masked dancer
hair shorn
notes & words & lines
& graphic eyes
eternity
the blink of an eye
a hOwling
a hYmn
wandering

ЖƎπƟπƎЖ

a boat
full sail

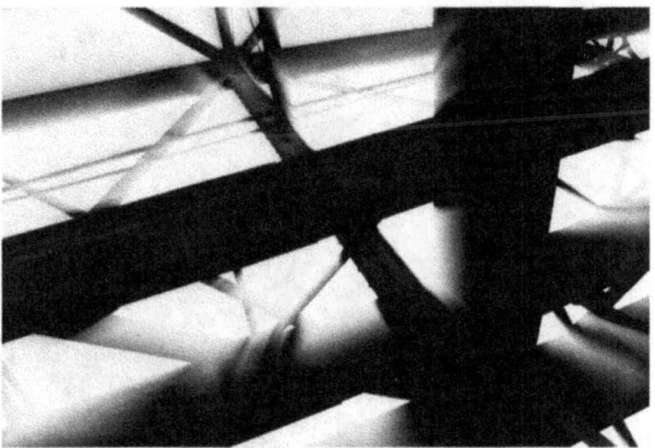

keel-furrowed
glides across
relentless waves
itself a wave
water & rocky cliff
glacial depths & seagulls' cries
or slender willow
flint, fire, glass
illumined — not far
but close

it was so hard in the beginning
rigging without motion
forced, scraped, awkward
but not a bird
not a long-necked bird
awkward but not beautiful
not twisting skyward
a flat failure — leaden
not grief
but a longing

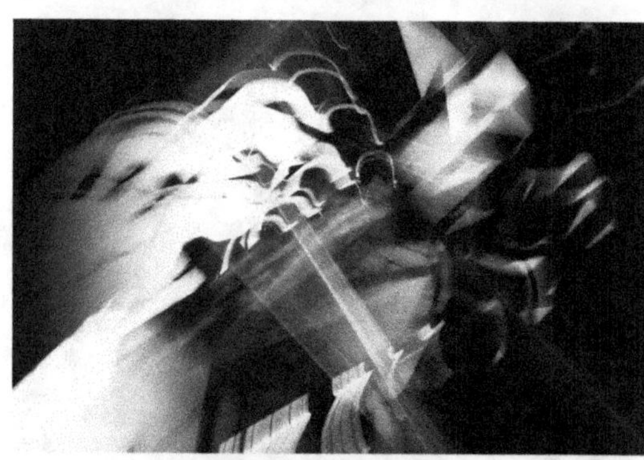

i first heard your voice
a swan
i reached towards you
my heart leapt towards you
dark angel
mine

wordless
wondrous swan
an endless climbing
hand over bow
wire & wood & sky

storm
wooden mast
splintered against the rock
not you but my wings
bone & sinew
so far to row
endless passage

resistance
a bird
but falling

ЖꟼπØπꟼЖ

there were maps
black stones thrown
across black wires
& graphite words
graphite numbers
graphite language
drifting smoke
across the worn
manuscript
5 line sea

there was
a room
with wooden cabinets
filled with maps
wooden floor
blackened floor
dusty light
storefront windows
cello maps
dead hands speaking
from fallen stones
this world
a note in a bottle
for cello
for viola
or oboe

other sections
other worlds

maps stuffed into drawers
hard to climb but
intoxicating views
a whole afternoon
finding footholds

touching tender stems
so far from rain & stone
to river

the measures
hammered
chiseled

hand to surface
small turns
smooth glass
twisted reach
ascension — then river
a scattering of ashes
dissolution
one thousand stars

ЖƏπØπƏЖ

between 2 deserts
berryman's dream
water, steel, sun

ЖƏπØπƏЖ

silence

not
silence

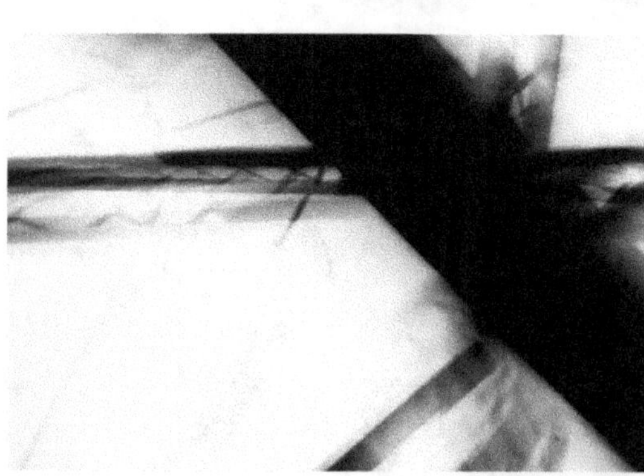

ghosts breathe
blankness
snow
an emptiness or forest
trace of birds
or cloud
or wind

silence

graphite line
drawn on

blank paper
frayed lines
shadow & light

graffiti tunnel
graffiti angel
night angel

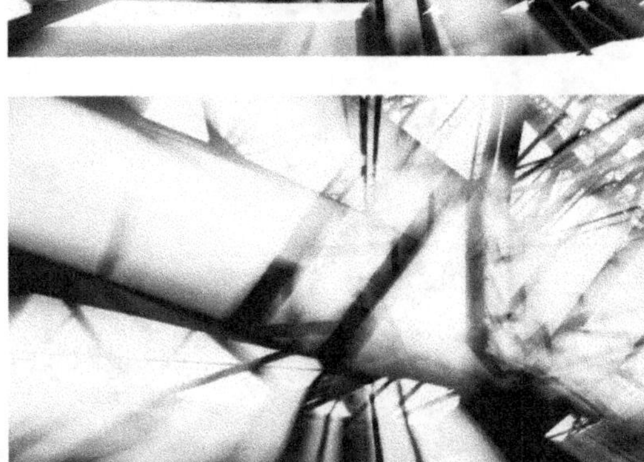

ЖↃπØπↃЖ

search for iron
broken compass
or hole in the sky
sky tunnel
cyclone sky
or sand or wolves or nest
warped compass
bent sound
bending trees or waves
slate blue cloud & sea
a wanderer
a stone

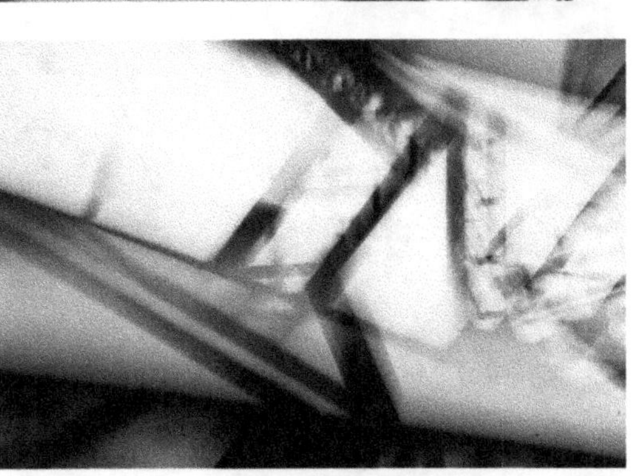

a cloth
the forge, the fire
the blacksmith
welding elements
fusing metals
now a pond
silent &
pensive
still water or
glass
not iron
brown jade
the color of sand
a simple sack of feathers
a frayed sack of feathers
threads woven into branches
& flight
wax wings
pale stone

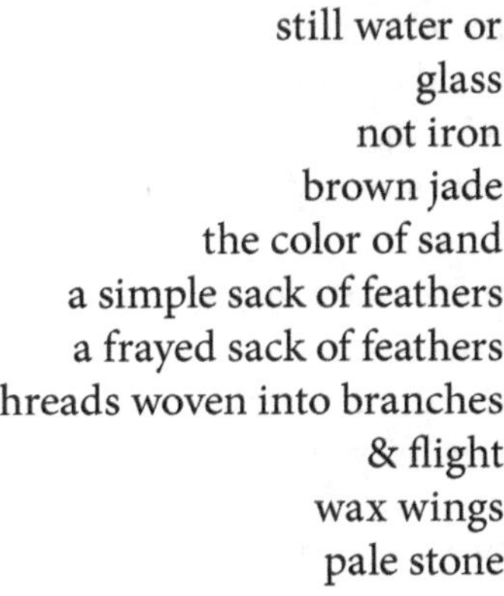

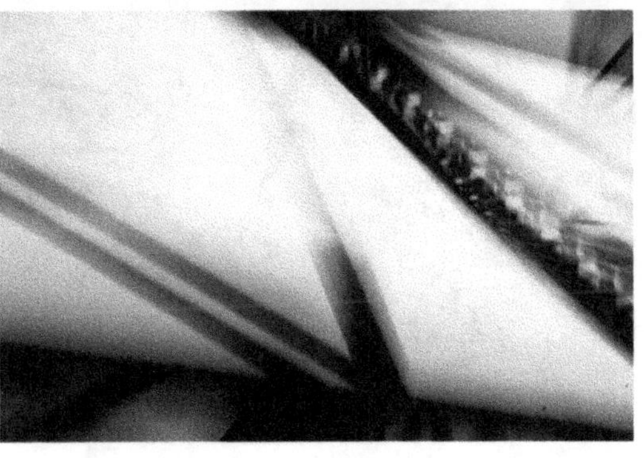

or cloud

ЖϿпϿпϿЖ

there was a door or heart
a cloud or white cloth
& wind
past mountains
an ancient glacier
stripped of ice
barren rock
worn smooth & pale
ghost stone
ghost cloth
ice dreams
infused with light
once soaked in cloud
now sand or
balding sun
cool moon
a nest of dreams
lost language
brief vision
lonely hands
a memory
extinction
ancient seagull's landing
ancient ship
thread & ink
the window, the dream
the cloud
flood of cloud
waning light
pale stone, pale cloth
far away
there was a glacier
now stone
there was a cloud
now frayed

ЖϿпϿпϿЖ

pond water & pale translucent stone
burlap woven & frayed
thread unfurled & drifting
hands

shadows
dimly lit & winter night
luminous morning
pale ice & summer green
cave cloth
not snow but rough grass
or glacial ice
not blue but smooth, pale surface
opaque & bending
surface slowly turning
textured — rough & smooth
infinite lily pads
lily pads spilling across canvas
infinite pond
& sky
water / pigment
elemental forms
water, stone, fabric
not lake but color
not iron but bone
stone like bone
ancient human
cloth or hair

or glacier

ЖꟼπØπꟼЖ

blue green marble
small planet

ЖꟼπØπꟼЖ

abstraction / between
queer
cello blue boat
boundless sea

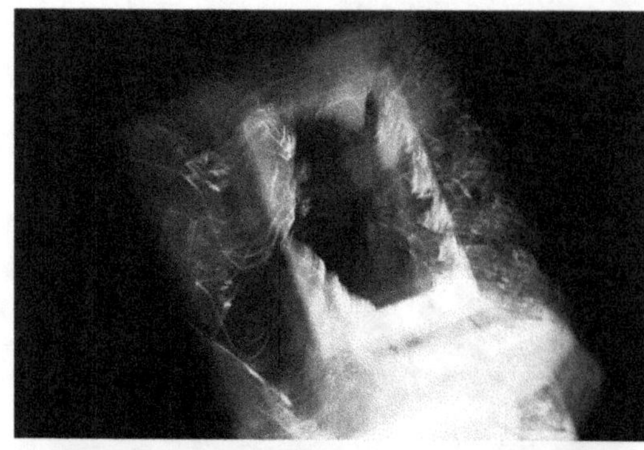

an intimate biography

the infinite between
the uncountably infinite
degenerate night crow
wandering
angels

the score
a circle of fire

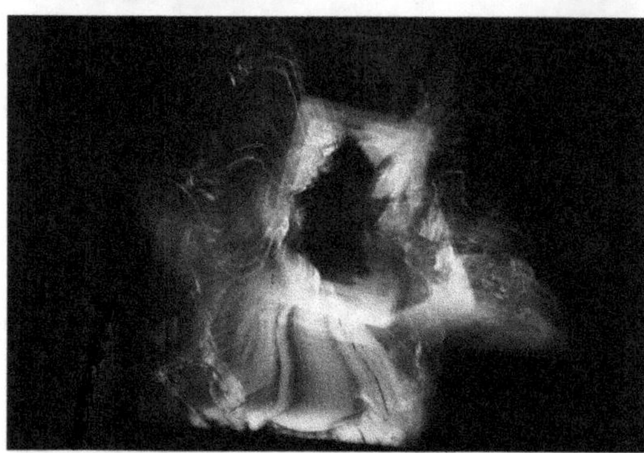

cello
glass bowl
coffeepot
rusted door
tuning fork
light, color
line, photos
echo, filters
contrast, echo, masking

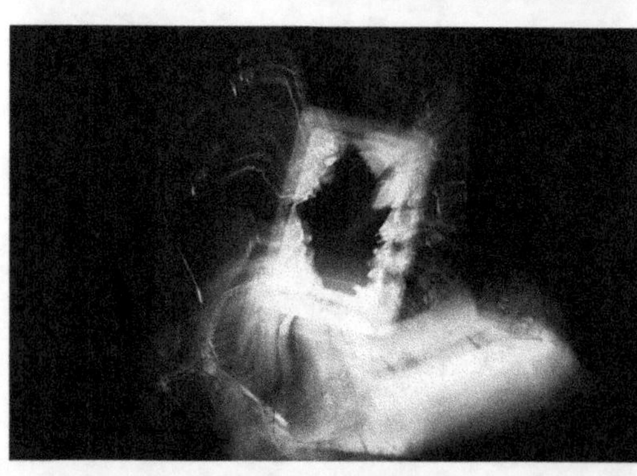

holy flight
holy dreaming
holy threads
holy rising
holy communion
holy echo
primal intertwine
awkward reaching
wings or streets
bridge or cloud
ascension, sea or sky

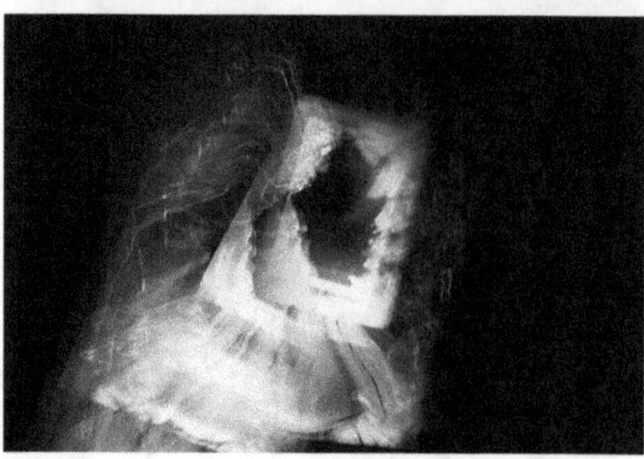

night crow on
percussion
setting something
into vibration
by rubbing
scraping
striking
shaking
sticks & membrane

wood & metal

colliding bodies
the acoustic
significance of material
cave tapping
cave drawing
resonance
painting
2 birds
last bird
& sea
far away remembered sea
vast & forever sea
scratching crow
story tapper
narrator crow
sea conjurer
magician
broken pump
pitch fraying / staining
pitch dissolving
wild bird, ancient bird
transfigured night
city bent on redemption
queer
glory
broken hYmn, falling sky
cathedral
warehouse
this room
this communion, this fusion
hands & breath, holy soul
holy planet, holy now
note frayed, tonal sky, sound cathedral
the past stains this place
wolf notes, awkward sky

city lights
crow blue sea or stairs
cloud cathedral or this room
only this gravity

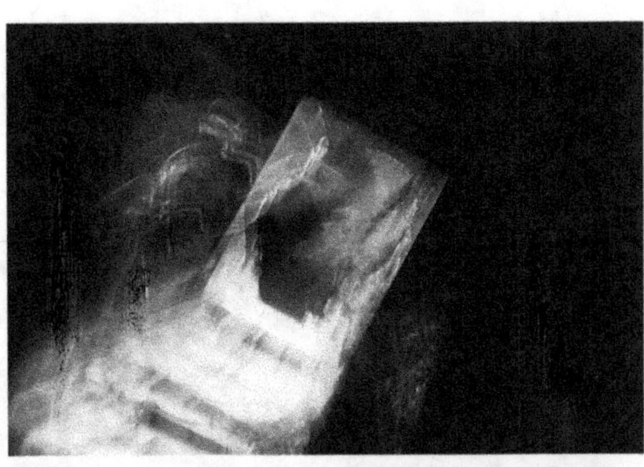
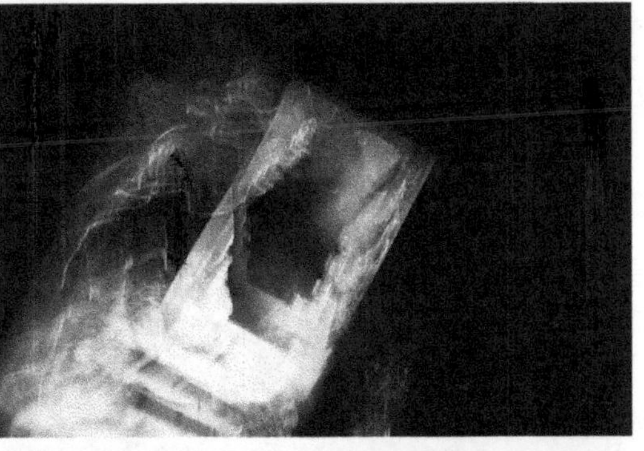
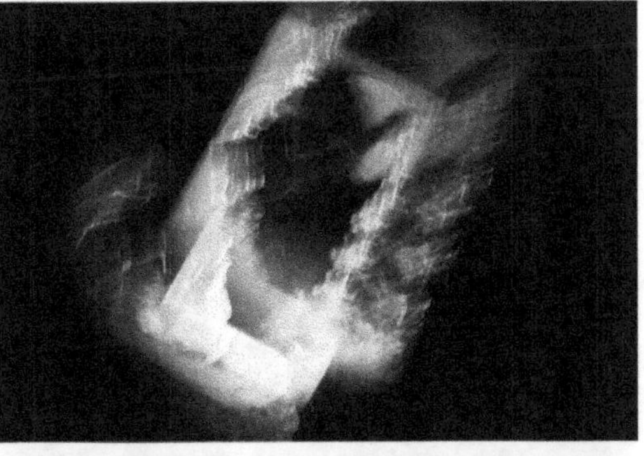
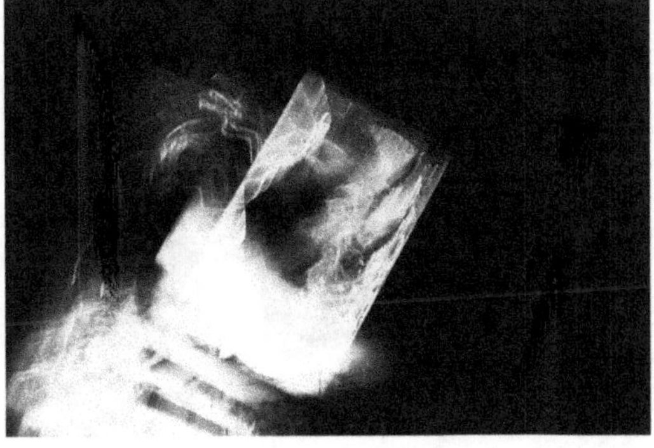

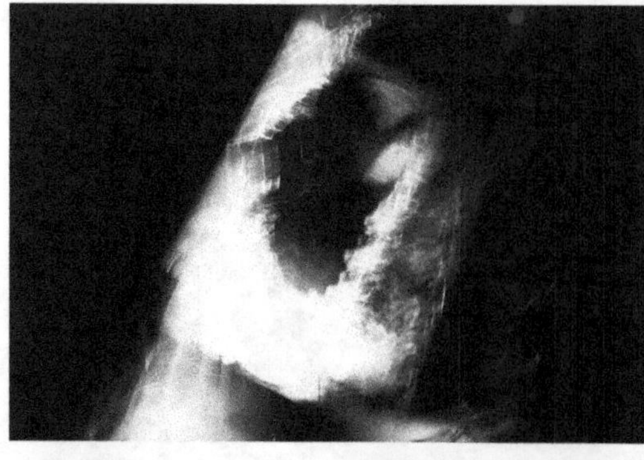

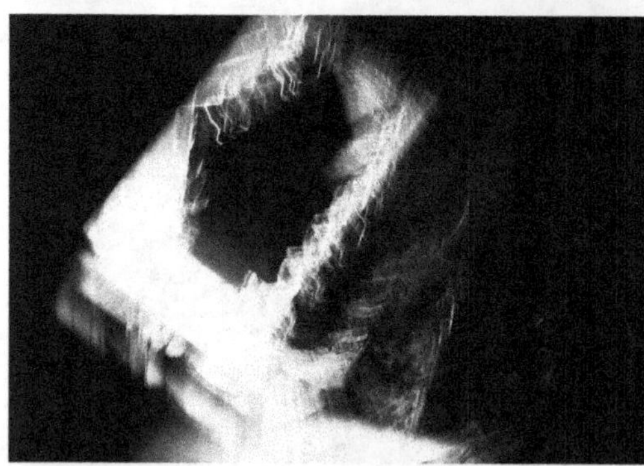

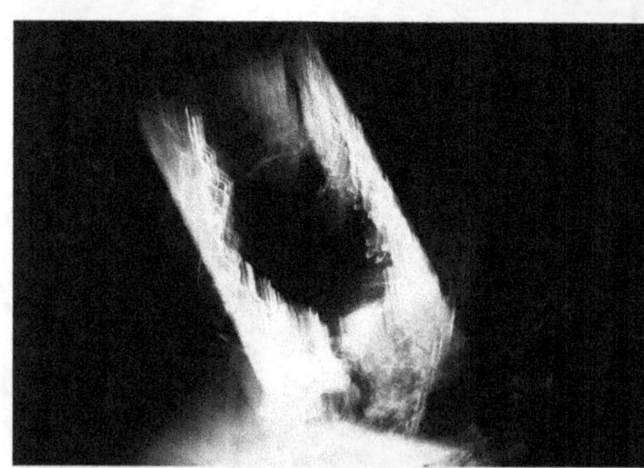

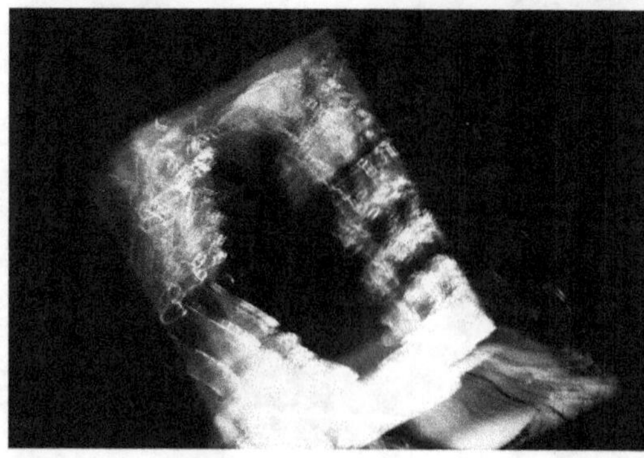

only this orbit
land resists
reed crow
this place a cloud
wax wings — suspended
bow or bone
feathers
beak or wood
missed connections
frayed
failing
missed migration, lost orbit
friction
angel
physics & pitch
night crow / courier / typographer
black ink
storyteller / magician / conjurer
witness
degenerate time
fragmented landscape
a tapping, a scraping
beer caps & prism eyes

ЖƐπØπƐЖ

you meant to
narrate or compose
or conduct this piece but
once again
the bright shiny object
the rock almost seemed
like language
you became a broken well
if you
tapped or rubbed
or scraped this place
this ocean could
draw water
you were going to play
the xylophone (pretty bones)
instead

industry! & glass bowl
singing
sparse, too preoccupied
to vibrate
near-sighted crow
black wings, black dots
black ink & lines
black scrawl
you were supposed to be the sea
black feathers askew
you were supposed to have
an orchestra
the loom, the frame
a concerto
the risks!
bow, friction, release
claw scraped wood & wire
harmonic ghosts
the infinite between
no boat
forces pull & resist
friction or flight
falling
ghost bird, shadow bird
you were supposed to have an orchestra
you were going to
play the marimba
be the sea
blue black sea

Ж϶πϴπ϶Ж

2 monologues, 2 soliloquies
twisted & frayed
rising vortex
communion of souls
concerto for stringed instrument
& bones
an alchemy of sea & flickering light
the color of honey
ancient papers
burlap threads

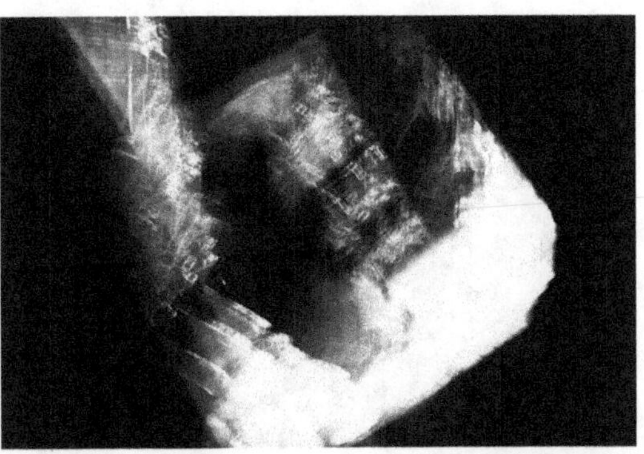
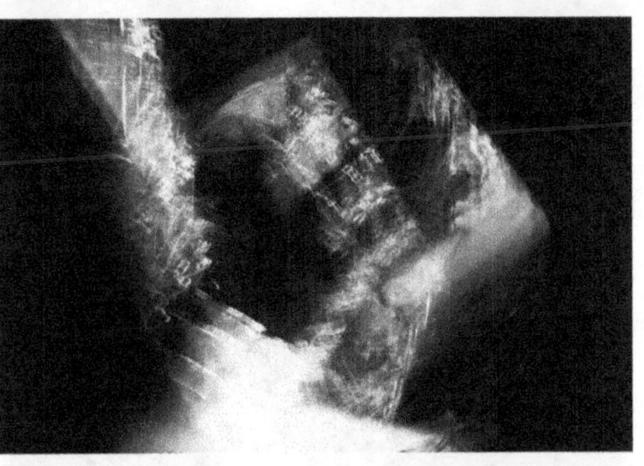
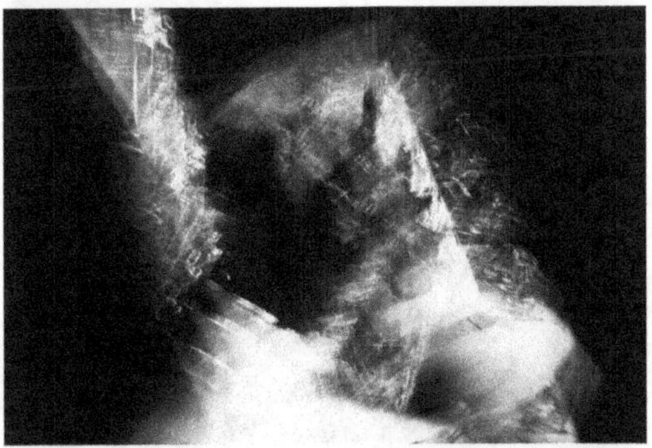
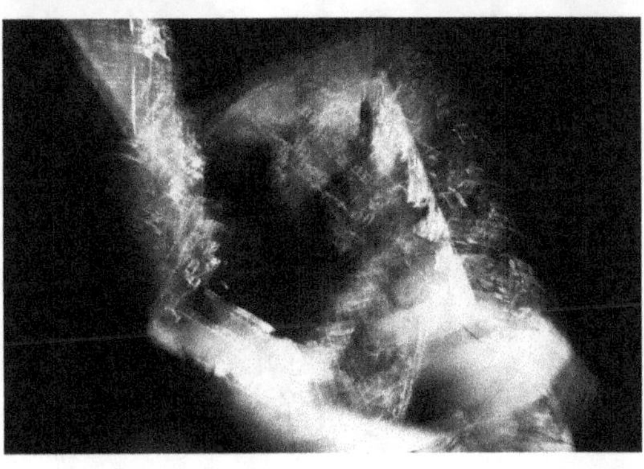

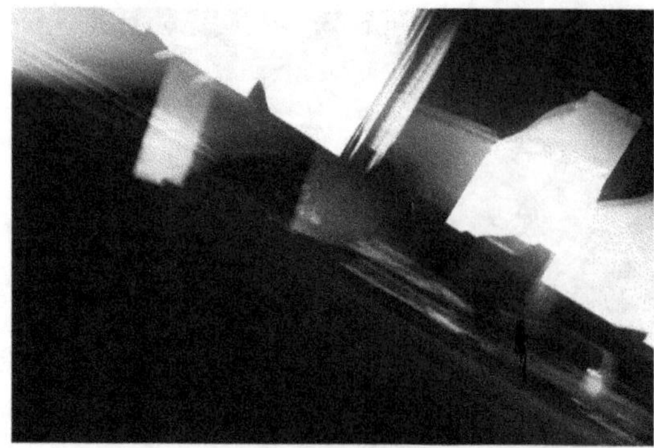

a sack
a floating crate
harmony
a collision
an elemental fusion
rhythm / a tapping / scratching
melody / a frayed call or hOwl
alchemical blurring
staining each other
sound & crow
moments & pitch clouds
flickering / fading
close / disoriented
vibrant / wild

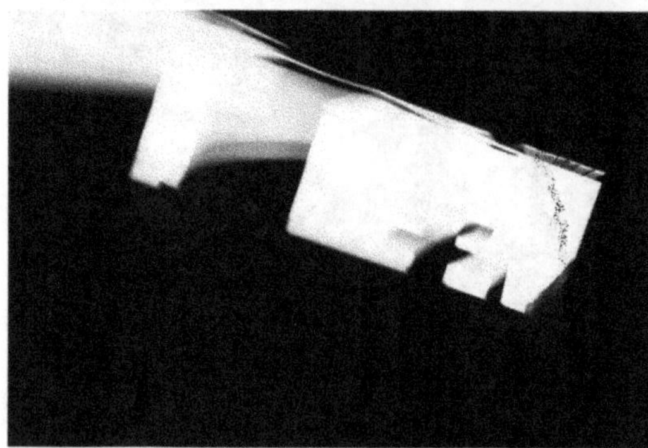

repeated arc
dense thicket
off-center
skewed
close
flight / redemption
transcendence
wanderer hOwl
luminous darkness
an impulse to flight
human resilience
the boat, the journey
sound fragments
like dreams

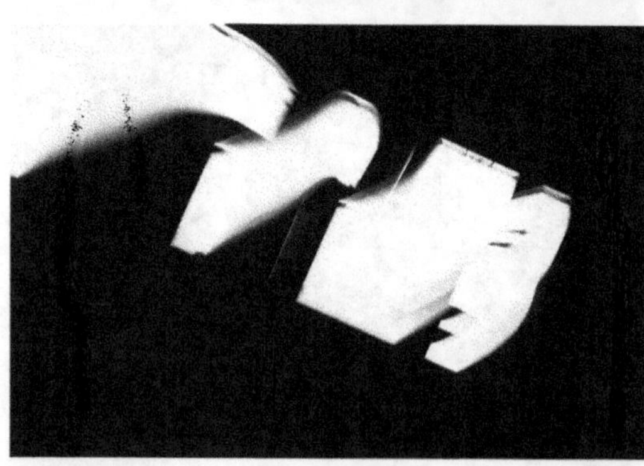

staring into each other
continuous pool
an edge, an intensity
abstract / gender / queer
lens / frame
skewed images
repeated
a boat
in the middle

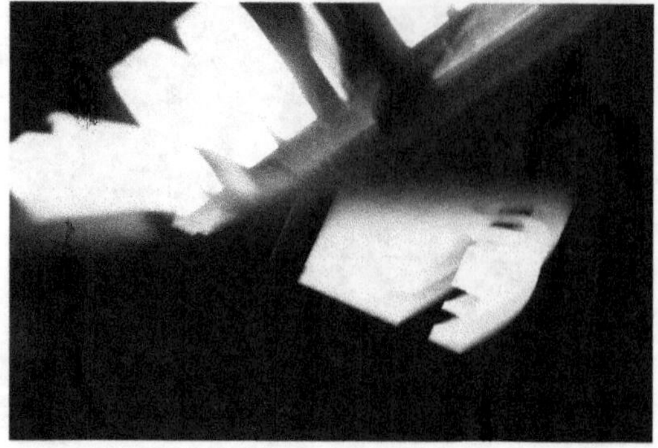

of the sea
horizon rocking
skewed
frameless world
a falling

or ascension
the ladder then

ЖↃπØπↄЖ

the data structure of dreams

episodic
glimpse
snapshot
& flow
a film

index of images
index of sound
index of dreams
graffiti / angel
scattered light & shadow

a blankness or silence
an emptiness
visual incident
the voyage out
revery
dream
a fever
waking
focal point / depth of field
stillness / runes
screens like quartets
or playing cards
shadow factory
light harp
bounds
twisting / reaching
rubbing / bending
a palette
a kite
silent manifesto
elemental forms
the boat, the wanderer, the sanctuary
manifest focal point

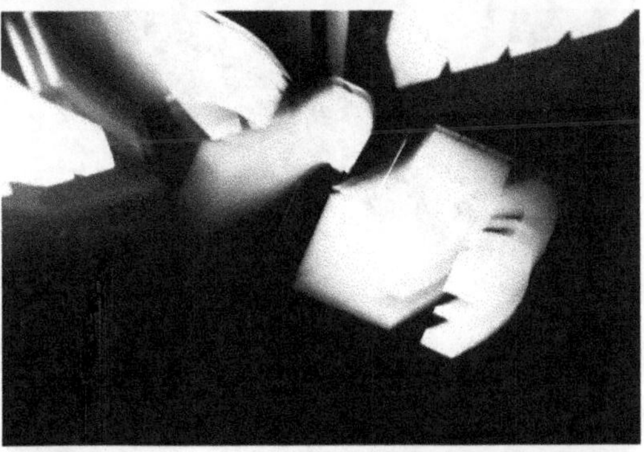

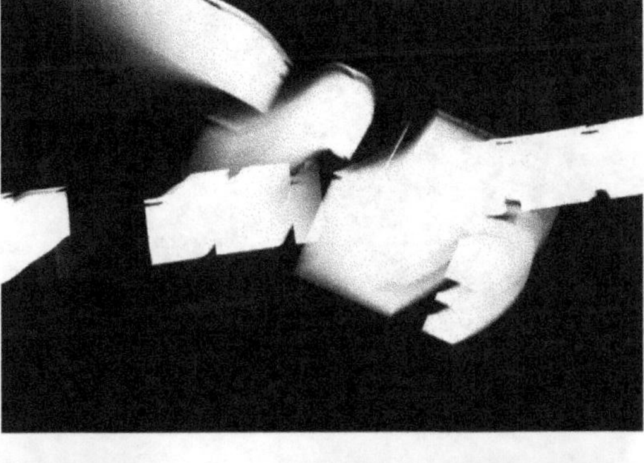

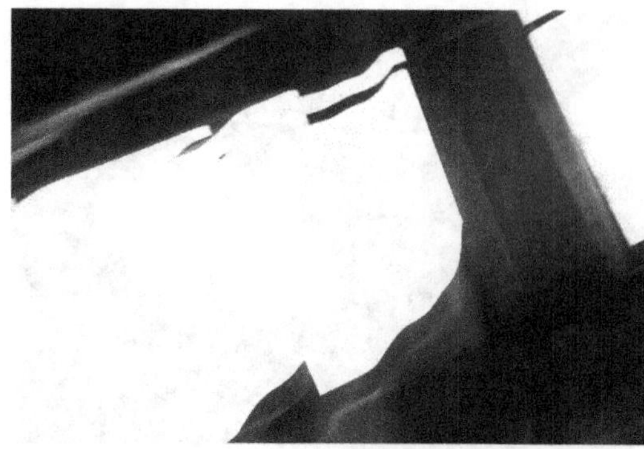

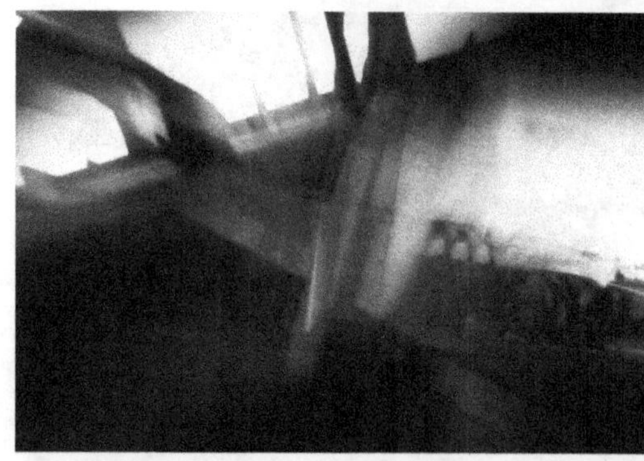

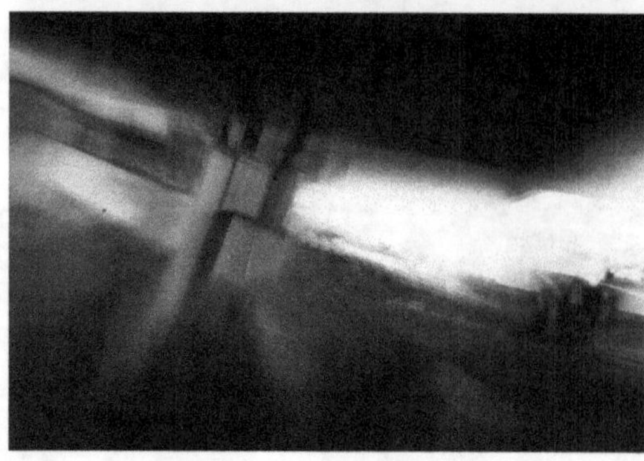

pivot point / inflection point
photosynthesis
wheel / fire
tonal pool
immersion
st. paul
tape delay
cello
graphite line
found sound
emergent hYmns
4 part 2 or 3
dissonance, friction
source
theater of eternal music
in the middle
a black music stand
lit
in darkness
shards
of broken glass
manuscript
drawing
frame to frame
found sound
collected sound
layered light
collage

sound clusters
gravity & tonal centers
kinetic forces
web or cloth
atmospheres
macro rhythms
a flow of moments
the rush of life / falling

mask
transmigration of souls
a cathedral of sound & light
aurally distant

long windows or arcs
film windows
blue windows
& sound sources
dissolve
& stain each other
create friction
& luminous union / chordal light
space & time migration
wanderers
holy fools
graffiti angel / the broken hYmns
graffiti angel / cave drawings
graffiti angel / house of light
graffiti angel / night train
graffiti angel / blue window

graffiti angel / hOwl
street lamp wanderer

ЖӬπØπӬЖ

grand gestures
faltering flight
it was like this every morning
the risks, the walls
the rejections
& simply
jumping
into
thin air

ЖӬπØπӬЖ

ocean, wind
& grief
ahab's dream

the gulf
breathe / oil

tar / feathers

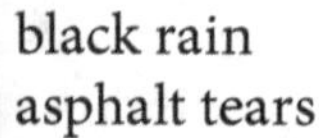
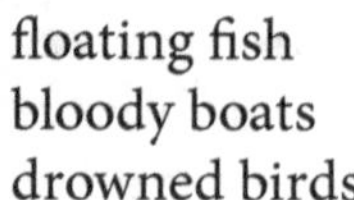

black rain
asphalt tears

floating fish
bloody boats
drowned birds

wire stitches
torn cloth
tattoo needle
neon cloth

my sister
strung out
nearly dead
went back to what hurt her
for the 4th time

i speak to you these words
i didn't know how to save her

she asked me to take photos
on the day
(she told me later)
she planned to die
i felt this somehow
even at the time
& had no other rope
to hold her
she wanted
a short film
shadow film
about / pain
you can construct a story
in so many ways
moving pictures
falling pictures
elegy or salvation
i didn't know how
to save her
but
she wanted to see

the final film

red lines
holy lines
broken mast
holy mast
torn sail
holy sail
foolish ahab
holy ahab
fool
holy fool

ЖƎπØπƎЖ

i was queer
transgender queer
& the planet was
dying
a heartless species
humans
i grew up to the sound of body counts
grainy black & white
television
evening news
it was like this every evening
rivers on fire
prisons
protests
wars
a white woman screaming
red-faced profanities
at a black girl
boarding a bus
nightly news
villages burning
orange balls of fire
in a jungle
gun to head
shutter / bang
image image image
& resistance

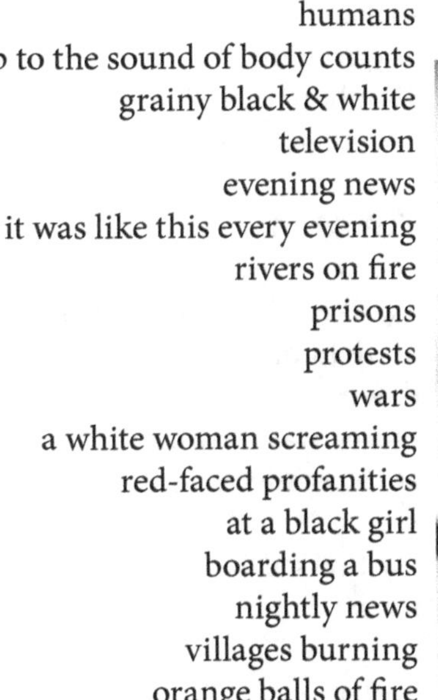

shutter / bang
eyes
fists
words
blood
tides
heart
of the beast
bowels
of the beast
helicopter blades
tents
liquid metal
graffiti walls
a billion for the bomb
food stamps for the baby
a prison cell for you
rivers on fire
locked factories
locked out
locked in
at gunpoint
17th hour dim light
a woman sews

ЖƎπØπƎЖ

i walked the queer streets
at night or
dawn
on my way to work
at the modern times cafe

i witnessed
i saw

brown bodies
pinned across cop cars
& worse
i witnessed
i testify
i saw

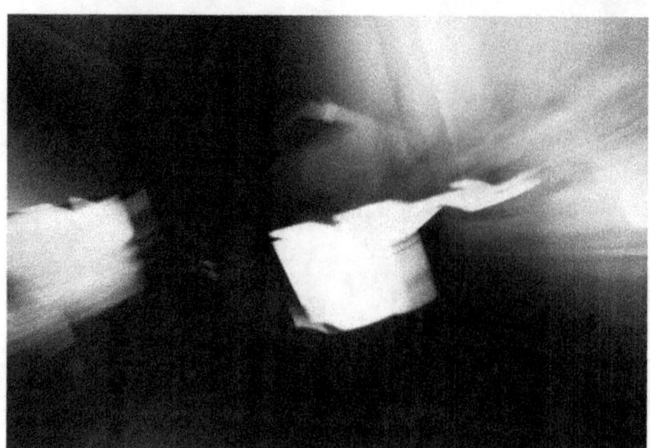

& called out
helpless

at night, at dawn
i walked the streets
paint for the bomb makers & porn shops
walking an invisible fluid line between
night is an angel
a neon prophet
suburban cars pausing for prostitutes
white boys
roaming in packs
searching out a stranger
alone & queer
to beat within an inch of his life
rites of manhood for the college set
neighborhood housing
projects
gaunt queer boys
coughing pretty boys
i walked the fluid line
between he & she
always queer
hey baby
i miss you

ЖϽπØπϽЖ

saxophones &
electrified
guitars
spilled from
summer open doors
flung windows
curl of smoke
rolling papers
lysergic dreams
i remember your eyes
green

ЖϽπØπϽЖ

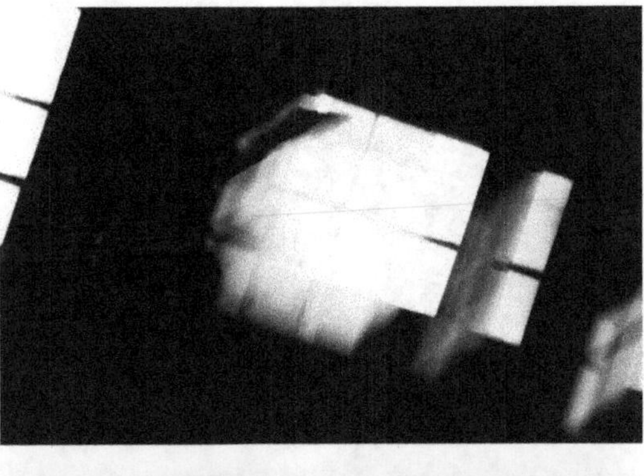
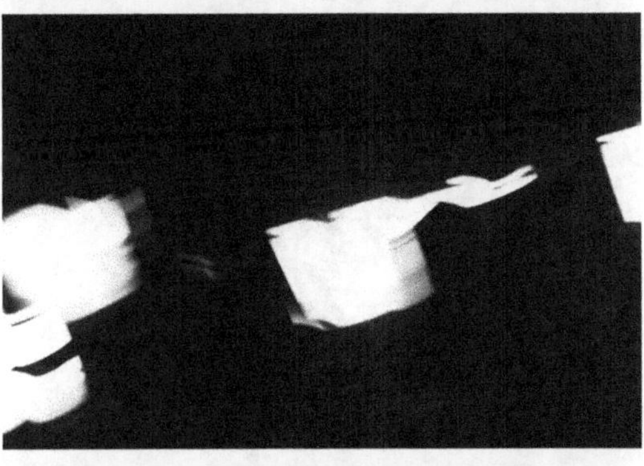
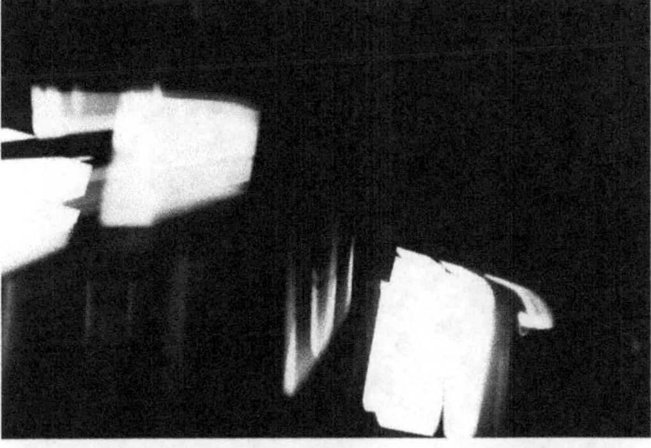
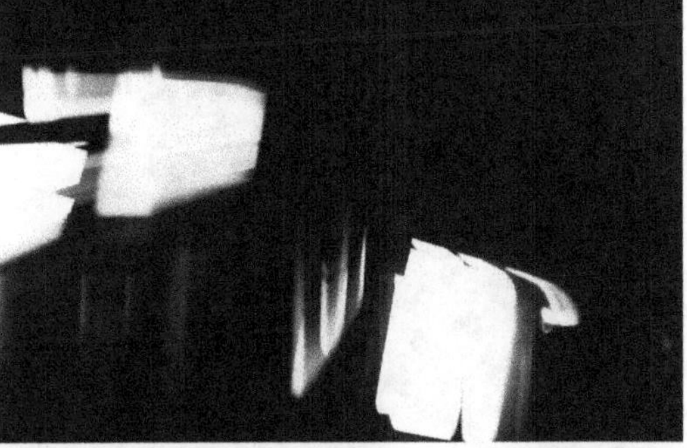
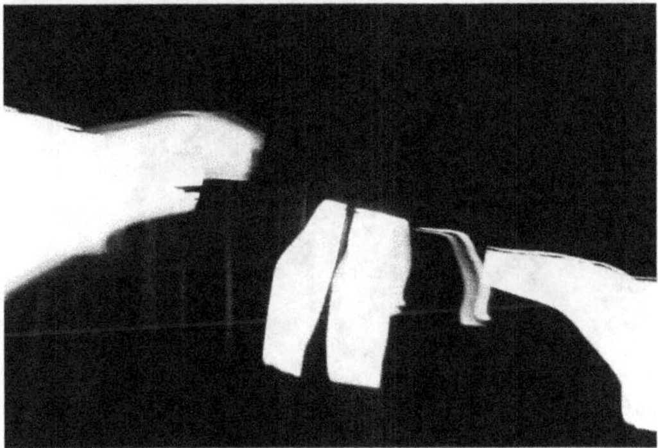

the saxophone player
from the psych ward
stunned out of
his mind
on some
psychotropic
tranquilizer
& yet
slow sweet sound
breath & reeds
burnished metal
hands & breath
sweet poet
shuffling poet
i remember you
in morning
awkward groups
sun through
metal bars
your words
sweet
kind
deranged
bent winged angel

ЖƎπØπƎЖ

& you 4 stringed lantern
wooden heart
my bones

i remember you
in hot practice rooms
hours & hours
& then forsaken
lost & forsaken bicycle
i can't even say it
can't tell you

lonely streets

wooden boat through

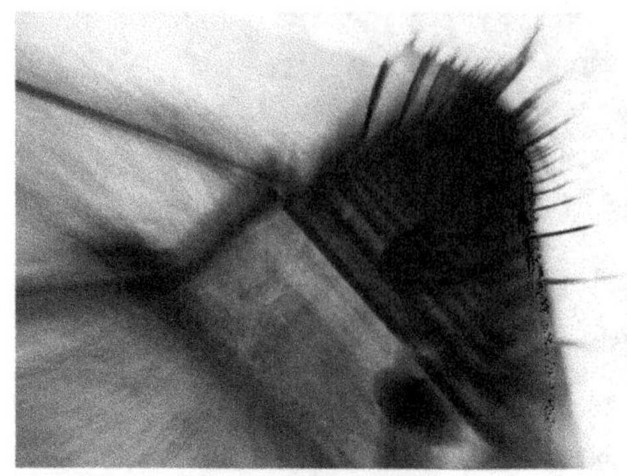

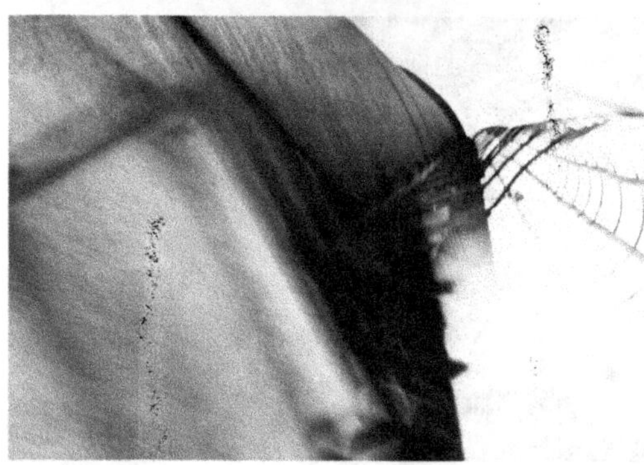

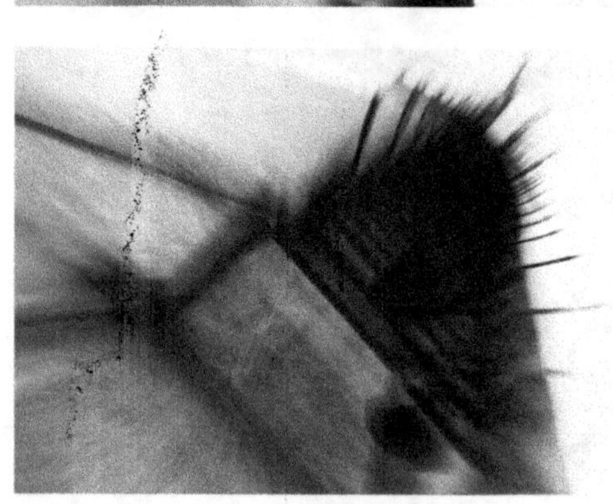

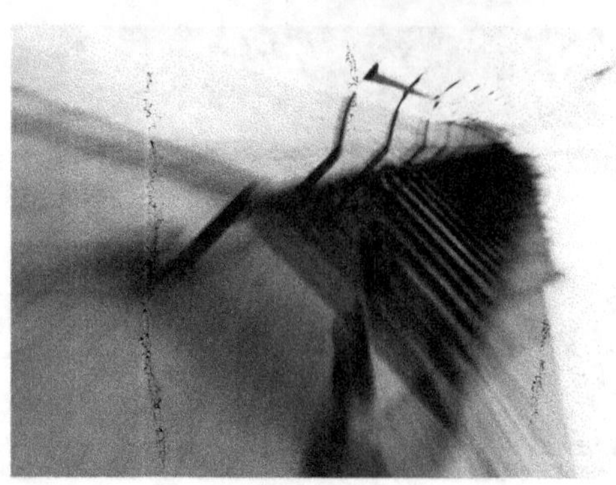

skipped school
don't talk about it school
bully school

frayed pitch
rough, raw, broken
strange beautiful pitch
resinous pitch
horse hair wire
wood
pine blood pitch
cat gut & wire
pitch

ЖƎπØπƎЖ

you have to fail 13 times
before you see the ladder
& even then
you can't reach
the last rung

ЖƎπØπƎЖ

frayed rope
musical line split
& frayed
& filtered
through water
contrast, color
filter, blur, echo
the canvas of
river & street

ЖƎπØπƎЖ

if it is in 2nd person
it is
a score

ЖƎπØπƎЖ

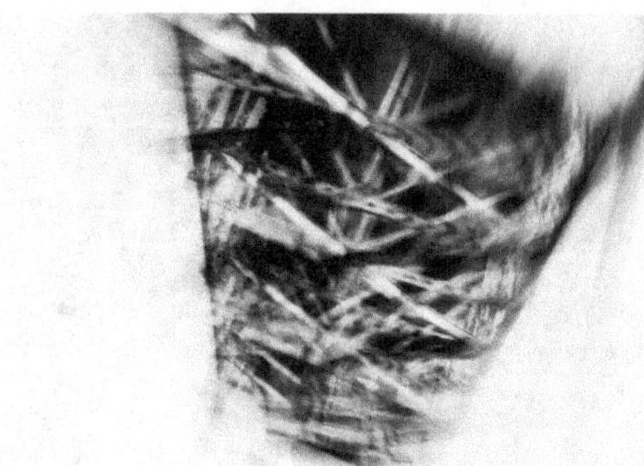

ЖƎпØпƎЖ

my hands were made of
ambiguity
geometry
a distance
a confluence
a mapless continuity
complicity & resistance
cluster of birds
pulse
a flux
atoms
carbon
dissipating
heat
or torch & ice
a glacier
drowning
in its own red sea
so difficult to utter
such grief

ЖƎпØпƎЖ

3 moons
skewed horizon
incoherence
near / far
unpinned
sound is like
a ragged line
stain of red
wash of ink

my hands were birds
no birds
my hands were rivers
no rivers
my hands were
bone & pulsing sound
a cacophony of horses
across blue sky

ЖƎпØпƎЖ

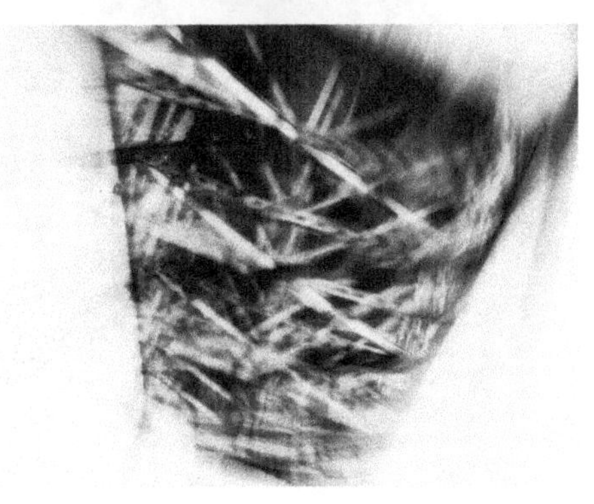

about my work

I am a cellist/composer/multimedia artist. In both live performance and recorded work, I blend cello, found sound, electronic effects and abstract, layered, still-motion film. The cello's ability to range from deep resonance to a ghostlike harmonic voice provides an expressive source for much of my multimedia work. My cross-sensory, blurred vision of the world impacts my visual language. I am inspired by emergent, organic forms, beat poets and abstract expressionist art. I use chance and generative forms to create sparse, minimalist spaces to dense, synesthetic, orchestral landscapes.

Using a multimedia approach, I engage in the quest to know, articulate, and grapple with the ephemeral, elusive underworld of our experience — the ways we construct our personal story, the relationship to our physical surroundings and the myths / ghosts that exist in that landscape.

Three years ago I was playing cello in a cafe on a summer evening. There was a dusty window beside me and the slanted rays of sunlight filtered through the glass in threads that I could see and hear — a palpable, chordal cross-sensory sound that stained my own playing. I have searched for that sound ever since. I often call that the broken hYmn. It is elusive, unknowable, ungraspable — a quest destined for failure — a worthy obsession — a reaching or longing.

I have grown to think of my work as a wandering narration — a lonely soliloquy by an abstract storyteller muttering in the darkness. I envision an infinite line — the drawing — the graffiti of sound and light that passes through our hand in the fleeting moment that we live on this earth — our imprint. The work then exists in a metaphysical dream world and manifests itself over time. I started reaching across the senses to create a sound / light polyphony — an immersive world. I blurred the borders between sight and sound and feeling — I started to let those boundaries fray. Light and sound waves are similar; I started thinking of the confluence as sine-wave orchestration.

Over time I have evolved from classical cello performance and composition to free-improvisational cello and sound art to cross-media sculpture / drawings / film / live performance. Still using the cello as source I now bend light and color into the mix. This is a new language for me. I am still working to integrate this cross-sensory language into an effective expressive voice. I am currently developing these "sound drawings" — exploring the dramatic potential of light, texture, color and sound as they unfold and intersect. This fusion space for me is sculptural — metaphorically similar to a mobile with intersecting, loosely-coupled components. I am interested in the relational dynamic between elements — the interactive friction and release, echo, resonance, fraying, and fissures.

My creative process involves first creating and recording found sound (from the cello and other environmental sources). These sound threads are then layered and filtered into a chance-infused polyphony of music. The film process starts with taking abstract, blurred, close, kinetic still photos. I work with these photos individually and together in a series, adjusting contrast and saturation, and masking image onto image (staining one image onto another to create a flow or a sense of falling). These composite, filtered images become frames in still-motion film clips. The clips are in turn layered much like the sound threads — to create a multi-threaded final film.

I am currently exploring the confluence of sound, image and word in different spatial and temporal landscapes — live, multimedia performance, cinema, the book, the hypertext web world. Each of these settings provides a different canvas or frame and shapes the resulting work / stains the expressive voice. Each of these physical manifestations exist at a different scale and level of interactivity for artist and viewer. A web presence is open-ended and caters to a wandering viewer. It facilitates a geographic freedom to share the work. The web or cloud world is like a box full of image, sound and word elements that can become a palette or set of sketches for the other forms. It is a sea navigable by hypertext maps. I call this space "blue boat." Visit www.cellodreams.com to explore this cloud world.

The cinematic form inhabits a self-contained, single-projection, linear time frame. It asks the artist to confront a linear arc / a single road from start to finish. The viewer is now accustomed to seeing narratives mapped onto this form. Experimental film can alter this expectation but it is clearly present for the viewer. I use distilled movement and sound — pulsing and dissolving frames, luminous color and shadow, a relentless musical flow, a rising, a falling, a twisting together of sound, light, elemental textures, and intersecting lines to create structure for film that is more closely related to musical forms.

Installation and live performance are juxtaposed with the physical environment, inter-twined with the space. I love to feel a room around me while I play — its resonance, ambience, quirky echoes and vibrations. One of my favorite spaces to play is at the Sacred Heart Music Center, an old cathedral in the heart of downtown Duluth. I love Sacred Heart for its beautiful, haunting resonance and fallen angel feel — a sense of decay and luminousness intermixed. From the rocky ledges that jut into the earthy underground of Sacred Heart to the organ loft, stained glass windows, and belfry there is an unmatched mix of color, texture, resonance, shadow and light. My cello loves it there — bird to ceiling / broken sky. Sanctified. Ascension.

Installation has a temporal framelessness. The artist doesn't control the viewer / the wanderer's experience. I like installation for its floaty immersion — the artist creates a pool or cloud for the viewer to drift through. Participants define their own window / their own path. The spatial aspect allows the artist to enfold the wanderer in a world of sound & light.

I have always been drawn to abstract art. I'm not a particularly cerebral person — I work more intuitively from my heart / eyes / ears / that feeling in the center of the chest.

There are several characters & landscapes that I loosely inhabit when I work. One is the city itself. I lived in Minneapolis for many years and traversed the city on foot, often walking for hours each day. The close, textured urban landscape influenced me deeply. When I am composing, the character or muse I call "graffiti angel" resonates the urban wanderer experience. Night crow / no time, the shiny-object black-winged muse, is the unreliable narrator. River icarus is another figure that took form while I was working on a commission from the American Composers Forum / Jerome Foundation. Tender-hearted icarus / the holy fool has a broken vulnerability, a dreaming self, a wax-wing self. They walk with me.

Kathy McTavish
November 2011

artist biography

Grants and Commissions (2009-2012):

2012 Jerome Foundation Commision
2011 Arrowhead Regional Arts Council Arts and Cultural Heritage Career Development Grant
2010 Arrowhead Regional Arts Council Arts and Cultural Heritage Individual Artist Fellowship
2009 American Composers Forum / Jerome Composers Commissioning Program
2009 Arrowhead Regional Arts Council / McKnight Foundation Artist Support Grant

Recent Multimedia Gallery Installations:

January 18-April 8, 2012: "Birdland" - Duluth Art Institute solo show (Duluth, Minnesota)
October 1-December 1, 2011: "Migrations / Lost & Forsaken Bicycles" - Phantom Galleries (Superior, Wisconsin)

Recent Multimedia Live Performance:
(live cello, recorded sound and abstract still-motion film projection)

October-November, 2011: "Migrations" - spoken word, cello and video projection at six venues throughout northern Minnesota and Wisconsin
June 8, 2011: "Light / Factory" - live music with multiple, integrated projections for the Sound Unseen Film Festival at Sacred Heart Music Center (Duluth, Minnesota)
May 17, 2011: "Last Bird & Sea" with Viv Corringham (voice) and Paul Cantrell (piano) for the American Composers Forum Salon at Studio Z (St. Paul, Minnesota)
February 27, 2011: "Women of the Kalevala: Skylark on a Stone" - spoken word, film and cello performance (with poets Sheila Packa, Kirsten Dierking, and Diane Jarvi) at the Open Eye Theater (Minneapolis, Minnesota)
April 22, 2011: "Fire / Bird" at Beaners Central (Duluth, Minnesota)
2010 series "River Icarus: Rusted Bridge / Deep Water": commissioned work for cello / film - September 18, 2010: Hennepin Avenue United Methodist Church (Minneapolis, Minnesota), October 16, 2010: Lyric Theater (Virginia, Minnesota), November 5, 2010: Sacred Heart Music Center (Duluth, Minnesota), November 10, 2010: Winona State University Studio Arts Department Drawing Session (during performance - Winona, Minnesota)
October 3, 2010: "Cloud Birds" - poetry, cello and film for the poet laureate inaugural reading by Sheila Packa at the Weber Auditorium (Duluth, Minnesota)
August 28, 2010: "Ladders / Windows" a collaboration with Adam Sippola at Teatro Zuccone (Duluth, Minnesota)

Film Festival Premiers:

Black Iris (2011) with poet Sheila Packa at the Vancouver Visible Verse Film Festival (Vancouver, British Columbia), Immersion (2010) with poet Sheila Packa shown at the Duluth Short Film Festival hosted by the Duluth Playground and at the Co-Kisser Poetry / Film Festival at the Minneapolis College of Art and Design October 2011, Birdland (2010) shown at the 2011 Free Range Film Festival (Wrenshall, Minnesota)

Scores for Film:

24 Postcards by Garrett Tiedemann (2011 - available online and soundtrack released through American Residue Records), "Hands" written for Life of Riley by 4-Track Films (2011), recorded + live sound for Vertov's 1929 Soviet silent film "Man with a Movie Camera" (2010 - shown at Duluth's Zinema 2).
Other: My work or the work of the Cosmic Pit Orchestra has been used behind a number of projects including those by Andy Underwood, (Walker Art Center Upside Down City by Claes Oldenburg, Walker Inside Out / Art Goes Outdoors: a celebration of the Minneapolis Sculpture Garden's 20th Anniversary), Marc Swoon Bildos Neys, Dudley Edmundson, Patrick Eller, Garrett Tiedemann and others.

Listing of Recorded Work:

cellodreams / solo cello: i was looking for you (2011), resistance (2011), compression: 60 seconds (2010 - for the 60x60 competition), bent / hOwl (2010), holy fool (2010), ahab's dream (2010 - recently used behind a local production of "Hamlet"), man with a movie camera film score (2010), the sound of everyday objects (2010), breathe / oil (2010), accordion music (2010), ocean | wind | grief (2010), iron, glass, noise (2010), what is 6 minutes? (2010), nyx (2010), radio pluto (2010), klikt / response (2010), river icarus: rusted bridge / deep water (2010), between2deserts /one (2010), between2deserts / the swan (2010), graffiti tunnel (2010), graffiti / 2 hands (2010), photosynthesis (2010), north sea (2009), subway icarus / last dream (2009), cloth (2008), winged instrument (2008), cave drawings (2008), love meditations (thematic collection, 2008), crane language (2008), the infinite between (2007), night language (2007), lines (2007), dusk filaments (2007), rain clouds (2007), summer 06 (2006), noise2peace (2006), 4 strings (2006), i meant to say (2006)

wildwood river / with poet Sheila Packa: correspondence 2: in translation (2011 - published in qarrtsiluni), correspondence 1: i said i (2011), undertow (2010), echo & lightning (2009), fearful journey (2008), dear bird (2006)

cosmic pit orchestra / with Richie Townsend on electric guitar: hOwL 1 (2009), edge of peace collection (2008), industrial collection (2008), red queen diaries (2007), caught you falling (2007), primordial dreaming (2007), dreamtime (2007), twisted & frayed (2006), grief & love (2006), gossiping dolphins (2006)

Short music films (abstract still-motion with music): tent city (2011), traces (2011), the ladder (2011), birdland / 2 (2011), anatomy (2011), blue ladder (2011), hole in the sky (2010), birdland / 1 (2011), a man was bending circuits (2011), red stairwell (2011), the elevator room (2011), fire (2011), sand (2010), black sea (2011), blue window (2011), heaven (2010), crane language (2010), sky (2011), it was like this every morning (2010), red accordion (2010), trains (2010), riot (2010)
Short poetry films (abstract still-motion with poetry by Sheila Packa): velocity (2011), two worlds (2011), eurydyce (2011), loom (2011), was it I (2011), celluloid afterlife (2011), black iris (published at movingpoems.com 2011), immersion (2010)

Areas of Study:

As a classical cellist I studied privately with Minnesota Orchestra cellists Anthony Elliot and Sachiya Isomura and studied piano performance, music theory and composition. I have a background in mathematics, ecology and music theory. The confluence of these research areas informs my work as a composer / multimedia artist. I create frameworks for representing dynamical systems and am interested in emergent structures, chance, myth, improvisatory forms, polyphony, interactive webs, harmonic relationships and the orchestration of sound, light, and color.

Formal Education:

Sign Language Interpreting Certificate - St. Paul Technical College
B.S. Mathematics - University of Minnesota, Duluth
M.S. Applied Mathematics (continuous modeling) - University of Minnesota
Ph.D. coursework in Theoretical Ecology (all but dissertation) - University of Minnesota

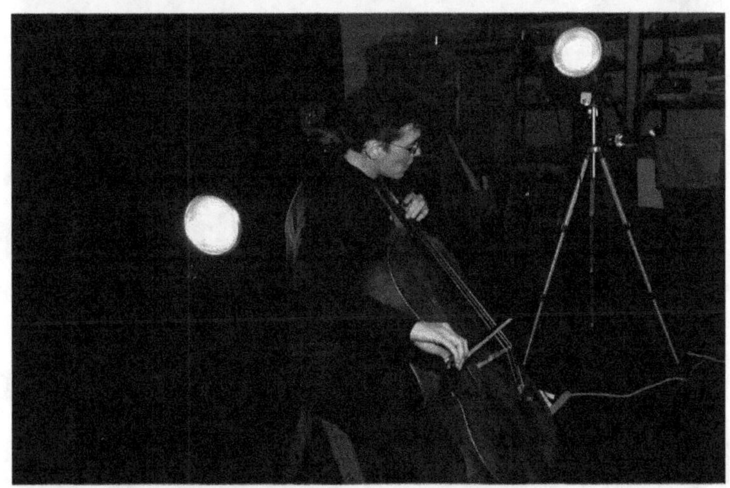

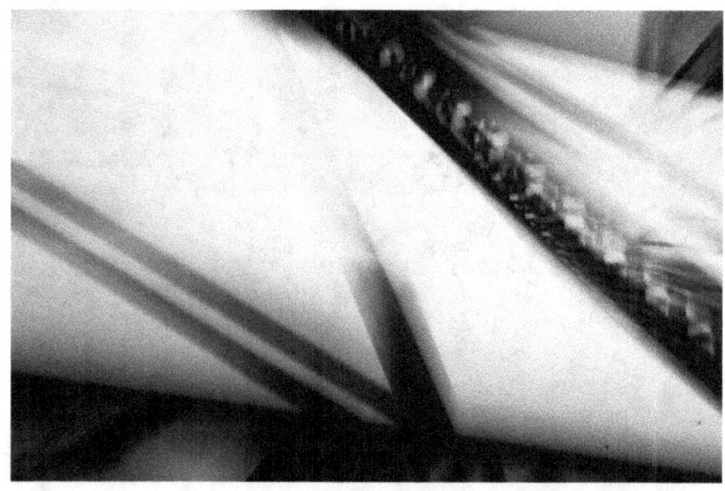

www.ingramcontent.com/pod-product-compliance
Lightning Source LLC
Chambersburg PA
CBHW080331030726
47593CB00010B/2965